WILLIAM JAMES
AND OTHER ESSAYS ON THE
PHILOSOPHY OF LIFE

WILLIAM JAMES
AND OTHER ESSAYS ON THE
PHILOSOPHY OF LIFE

BY

JOSIAH ROYCE, LL.D., Litt.D.

PROFESSOR OF THE HISTORY OF PHILOSOPHY
AT HARVARD UNIVERSITY

WIPF & STOCK · Eugene, Oregon

Wipf and Stock Publishers
199 W 8th Ave, Suite 3
Eugene, OR 97401

William James and Other Essays on the Philosophy of Life
By Royce, Josiah
Softcover ISBN-13: 978-1-7252-9924-5
Hardcover ISBN-13: 978-1-7252-9925-2
eBook ISBN-13: 978-1-7252-9926-9
Publication date 2/1/2021
Previously published by The Macmillan Company, 1912

This edition is a scanned facsimile of
the original edition published in 1912.

PREFACE

In previous works, and most systematically in the two volumes entitled "The World and the Individual," I have set forth and defended a form of philosophical Idealism. The essays collected in the present volume contain further illustrations and applications of this doctrine. They are all papers prepared for special occasions. The earliest in order of time was written in 1906. The latest, my address upon William James, was prepared in June of the present year. Each one of these essays can be understood independently. The justification for bringing them together in a single volume is expressed by the phrase "philosophy of life," used on my title-page. That is, each essay contains an interpretation of some problem that is, in my opinion, of vital interest for any one who

PREFACE

wants to form sound ideals for the conduct of life.

The discourse upon William James deals with some of his ideals, and incidentally indicates my own. The address upon recent discussions of the problems of truth explains why I cannot accept some of the positions of recent pragmatism, and why the frequent identification of the idealistic theory of truth with "barren intellectualism" appears to me erroneous. Since, in my opinion, the intellect and the will, logic and life, reason in the formation of ideas and reason in the guidance of conduct, have extremely intimate relations, which some recent discussions have both richly illustrated and waywardly obscured, the review of the problem of truth, although the most technical of the papers in this volume, seems to me to concern an issue that is as practical and vital as any other. As to the defense of the concept of "absolute truth" which the paper contains, I may at once say that "the absolute" seems to me personally not something remote, unpractical,

PREFACE

inhuman, but the most pervasive and omnipresent and practical, as it is also the most inclusive of beings. "Absolute truth" has therefore a distinctly and intensely practical import.

Of the other essays, the one on Christianity is a fragment of a study that I propose to carry out more fully at an early date. The essay on "Loyalty and Insight" summarizes the position that I have defended and illustrated in my "Philosophy of Loyalty," published in 1908, and brings the ethical doctrine there presented into touch with metaphysical idealism by means of a very summary indication of the thought which we owe to Kant's "Deduction of the Categories." How near that thought also is to the vital interests of daily life, I am never weary of trying to illustrate at a time when it is fashionable in this country to belittle the office of thought, and to make light of Kant.

The final discourse on "Immortality" approaches the familiar problem in a fashion different from that chosen for the purposes of

PREFACE

my "Ingersoll lecture" on the same topic (published by the Riverside Press in 1900), and thus forms a sort of supplement to the Ingersoll lecture. The present way of dealing with the concept of immortality also gives me the opportunity to sketch anew some of my general idealistic theses, and incidentally to repudiate the frequent and groundless assertion that my own form of idealism regards time as "unreal," or the absolute as "timeless," or the universe as a "block."

Since each of these papers is intended to be comprehensible by itself, I am obliged, in each, to state, more or less dogmatically, opinions which I have discussed and attempted to justify in former writings. Dogma, as such, has no place in philosophy. But the present book is no systematic treatise; and is to be judged, I hope, in the light of its own decidedly practical purpose, and of its accompanying limitations.

I have ventured to make the honored name of William James part of my title. The first

PREFACE

essay is a tribute to his memory. The others show, I hope, that, if I often oppose his views, I owe to him, as teacher, and as dear friend, an unfailing inspiration, far greater than he ever knew, or than I can well put into words.

JOSIAH ROYCE.

CAMBRIDGE, MASS.
 OCT. 5, 1911.

CONTENTS

ESSAY I

WILLIAM JAMES AND THE PHILOSOPHY OF LIFE   PAGE 3

ESSAY II

LOYALTY AND INSIGHT 49

ESSAY III

WHAT IS VITAL IN CHRISTIANITY? . . . 99

ESSAY IV

THE PROBLEM OF TRUTH IN THE LIGHT OF RECENT DISCUSSION 187

ESSAY V

IMMORTALITY 257

ESSAY I

WILLIAM JAMES AND THE PHILOSOPHY OF LIFE

ESSAY I

WILLIAM JAMES AND THE PHILOSOPHY OF LIFE[1]

FIFTY years since, if competent judges were asked to name the American thinkers from whom there had come novel and notable and typical contributions to general philosophy, they could in reply mention only two men — Jonathan Edwards and Ralph Waldo Emerson. For the conditions that determine a fair answer to the question, "Who are your representative American philosophers?" are obvious. The philosopher who can fitly represent the contribution of his nation to the world's treasury of philosophical ideas must first be one who thinks for himself, fruitfully, with true independence, and with successful inventiveness, about problems of philosophy. And, secondly, he must be a man who gives utterance to philosophical ideas

[1] Phi Beta Kappa Oration delivered at Harvard University, June, 1911.

which are characteristic of some stage and of some aspect of the spiritual life of his own people. In Edwards and in Emerson, and only in these men, had these two conditions found their fulfillment, so far as our American civilization had yet expressed itself in the years that had preceded our civil war. Edwards, in his day, made articulate some of the great interests that had molded our early religious life. The thoughts which he most discussed were indeed, in a sense, old, since they largely concerned a traditional theology. Yet both in theology and general philosophy, Edwards was an originator. For he actually rediscovered some of the world's profoundest ideas regarding God and humanity simply by reading for himself the meaning of his own religious experience. With a mysterious power of philosophical intuition, even in his early youth, he observed what, upon the basis of what we know to have been his range of philosophical reading, we could not possibly have expected him to observe. If the sectarian theological creed that he defended was to our minds narrow, what he himself saw was very far-reaching and profound. For he viewed religious problems with synoptic vision that enabled him to reconcile, in his own personal way, some of the greatest and most tragic conflicts of the spiritual world, and what he had to say consequently far transcended the interests of the special theological issues which he discussed. Meanwhile, he spoke not merely as a thinker, but as one who gave voice to some of the central motives and interests of our colonial religious life. Therefore he was, in order of time, the first of our nationally representative philosophers.

Another stage of our civilization — a later phase of our national ideals — found its representative in Emerson. He too was in close touch with many of the world's deepest thoughts concerning ultimate problems. Some of the ideas that most influenced him have their far-off historical origins in oriental as well as in Greek thought, and also their nearer foreign sources in modern European philosophy. But he transformed whatever he assimilated. He invented upon the basis of his personal experience, and so he was himself no disciple of the orient, or of Greece, still less of England and of Germany. He thought, felt, and spoke as an American.

Fifty years ago, I say, our nation had so far found these two men to express each his own stage of the philosophy of our national civilization. The essence of a philosophy, in case you look at it solely from a historical point of view, always appears to you thus: A great philosophy expresses an interpretation of the life of man and a view of the universe, which is at once personal, and, if the thinker is representative of his people, national in its significance. Edwards and Emerson had given tongue to the meaning of two different stages of our American culture. And these were thus far our only philosophical voices.

To-day, if we ask any competent foreign critic of our philosophy whether there is any other name to be added to these two classic American philosophers, we shall receive the unanimous answer: "There is to-day a third representative American philosopher. His name is William James." For James meets the two conditions just mentioned. He has thought for himself, fruitfully, with true independence, and with successful inventiveness. And he has given utterance to ideas which are characteristic of a stage and of an aspect of the spiritual life of this people. He, too, has been widely and deeply affected by the history of thought. But he has reinterpreted all these historical influences in his own personal way. He has transformed whatever he has assimilated. He has rediscovered whatever he has received from without; because he never could teach what he had not himself experienced. And, in addition, he has indeed invented effectively and richly. Moreover, in him certain characteristic aspects of our national civilization have found their voice. He is thus the third in the order of time among our representative American philosophers. Already, within a year of his death, he has begun to acquire something of a classic rank and dignity. In future this rank and dignity will long increase.

In one of James's latest utterances he indeed expressed, with characteristic energy, a certain abhorrence of what he called classical tendencies in philosophical thought. But I must repeat the word: Fortune not unjustly replies, and will reply to James's vigorous protest against every form of classicism, by making him a classic.

Thus, then, from the point of view of the competent foreign students of our philosophy, the representative American philosophers are now three and only three — Edwards, Emerson, James.

And of these three there can be little question that, at the present time, the most widely known abroad is James. Emerson has indeed found a secure place in the minds of the English-speaking lovers of his type of thought everywhere; and has had an important part in the growth of some modern German tendencies. But James has already won, in the minds of French, of German, of Italian, and of still other groups of foreign readers, a position which gives him a much more extended range of present influence than Emerson has ever possessed.

It is my purpose, upon the present occasion, to make a few comments upon the significance of William James's philosophy. This is no place for the discussion of technical matters. Least of all have I any wish to undertake to decide, upon this occasion, any controversial issues. My intentions as I address you are determined by very simple and obvious considerations. William James was my friend from my youth to the end of his beneficent life. I was once for a brief time his pupil. I long loved to think of myself as his disciple; although perhaps I was always a very bad disciple. But now he has just left us. And as I address you I remember that he was your friend also. Since the last annual meeting of this assembly he has been lost to us all. It is fitting that we should recall his memory to-day. Of personal reminiscences, of biographical sketches, and of discussions relating to many details of his philosophy, the literature that has gathered about his name during the few months since we lost him has been very full. But just as this is no occasion for technical discussion of his philosophy, so too I think this is no place to add new items to the literature of purely personal reminiscence and estimate of James. What I shall try to do is this: I have said that James is an American philosopher of classic rank, because he stands for a stage in our national self-consciousness — for a stage with which historians of our national mind must always reckon. This statement, if you will permit, shall be my text. I shall devote myself to expounding this text as well as I can in my brief time, and to estimating the significance of the stage in question, and of James's thought in so far as it seems to me to express the ideas and the ideals characteristic of this phase of our national life.

I

In defining the historical position which William James, as a thinker, occupies, we have of course to take account, not only of national tendencies, but also of the general interests of the world's thought in his time. William James began his work as a philosopher, during the seventies of the last century, in years which were, for our present purpose, characterized by two notable movements of world-wide significance. These two movements were at once scientific in the more special sense of that term, and philosophical in the broad meaning of that word. The first of the movements was concerned with the elaboration — the widening and the deepening — of the newer doctrines about evolution. This movement had indeed been preceded by another. The recent forms of evolutionary doctrine, those associated with the names of Darwin and of Spencer, had begun rapidly to come into prominence about 1860. And the decade from 1860 to 1870, taken together with the opening years of the next decade, had constituted what you may call the storm-and-stress period of Darwinism, and of its allied tendencies, such as those which Spencer represented. In those years the younger defenders of the new doctrines, so far as they appealed to the general public, fought their battles, declared their faith, out of weakness were made strong, and put to flight the armies of the theologians. You might name, as a closing event of that storm-and-stress period, Tyndall's famous Belfast address of 1874, and the warfare waged about that address. Haeckel's early works, some of Huxley's most noted polemic essays, Lange's "History of Materialism," the first eight or nine editions of Von Hartmann's "Philosophy of the Unconscious," are documents characteristic of the more general philosophical interests of that time. In our country, Fiske's "Cosmic Philosophy" reflected some of the notable features that belonged to these years of the early conquests of evolutionary opinion.

Now in that storm-and-stress period, James had not yet been before the public. But his published philosophical work began with the outset of the second and more important period of evolutionary thought — the period of the widening and deepening of the new ideas. The leaders of thought who are characteristic of this second period no longer spend their best efforts in polemic in favor of the main ideas of the newer forms of the doctrine of evolution. In certain of its main outlines — outlines now extremely familiar to the public — they simply accept the notion of the natural origin of organic forms and of the general continuity of the processes of development. But they are concerned, more and more, as time goes on, with the deeper meaning of evolution, with the study of its factors, with the application of the new ideas to more and more fields of inquiry, and, in case they are philosophers, with the reinterpretation of philosophical traditions in the light of what had resulted from that time of storm and stress.

James belongs to this great second stage of the evolutionary movement, to the movement of the elaboration, of the widening and deepening of evolutionary thought, as opposed to that early period of the storm and stress. We still live in this second stage of evolutionary movement. James is one of its most inventive philosophical representatives. He hardly ever took part in the polemic in favor of the general evolutionary ideas. Accepting them, he undertook to interpret and apply them.

And now, secondly, the period of James's activity is the period of the rise of the new psychology. The new psychology has stood for many other interests besides those of a technical study of the special sciences of the human and of the animal mind. What is technical about psychology is indeed important enough. But the special scientific study of mind by the modern methods used in such study has been a phase and a symptom of a very much larger movement — a movement closely connected with all that is most vital in recent civilization, with all the modern forms of nationalism, of internationalism, of socialism, and of individualism. Human life has been complicated by so many new personal and social problems, that man has needed to aim, by whatever means are possible, towards a much more elaborate knowledge of his fellow man than was ever possible before. The results of this disposition appear in the most widely diverse sciences and arts. Archæology and ethnology, history and the various social sciences, dramatic art, the novel, as well as what has been called psychical research — in a word, all means, good and bad, that have promised either a better knowledge of what man is or a better way of portraying what knowledge of man one may possess — have been tried and molded in recent times by the spirit of which recent technical psychology is also an expression. The psychological movement means then something that far transcends the interests of the group of sciences to which the name psychology now applies. And this movement assumed some of its most important recent forms during the decade in which James began to publish his work. His own contributions to psychology reflect something of the manifoldness and of the breadth of the general psychological movement itself. If he published the two great volumes entitled "Psychology," he also wrote "The Varieties of Religious Experience," and he played his part in what is called "psychical research."

These then are James's two principal offices when you consider him merely in his most general relations to the thought of the world at large in his time. He helped in the work of elaborating and interpreting evolutionary thought. He took a commanding part in the psychological movement.

II

But now it is not of these aspects of James's work, significant as they are, that I have here especially to speak. I must indeed thus name and emphasize these wider relations of his thought to the world's contemporary thought. But I do so in order to give the fitting frame to our picture. I now have to call attention to the features about James which make him, with all his universality of interest, a representative American thinker. Viewed as an American, he belongs to the movement which has been the consequence, first, of our civil war, and secondly, of the recent expansion, enrichment, and entanglement of our social life. He belongs to the age in which our nation, rapidly transformed by the occupation of new territory, by economic growth, by immigration, and by education, has been attempting to find itself anew, to redefine its ideals, to retain its moral integrity, and yet to become a world power. In this stage of our national consciousness we still live, and shall plainly have to live for a long time in the future. The problems involved in such a civilization we none of us well understand; least of all do I myself understand them. And James, scholar, thinker, teacher, scientific and philosophical writer as he was, has of course only such relation to our national movement as is implied by the office that he thus fulfills. Although he followed with keen interest a great variety of political and social controversies, he avoided public life. Hence, he was not absorbed by the world of affairs, although he was always ready to engage generously in the discussion of practical reforms. His main office with regard to such matters was therefore that of philosophical interpreter. He helped to enlighten his fellows as to the relations between the practical problems of our civilization and those two world-wide movements of thought of which I have just spoken.

Let me call attention to some of the results of James's work as interpreter of the problems of the American people. I need not say that this work was, to his own mind, mainly incidental to his interest in those problems of evolutionary thought and of psychology to which I just directed your attention. I am sure that James himself was very little conscious that he was indeed an especially representative American philosopher. He certainly had no ambition to vaunt himself as such. He worked with a beautiful and hearty sincerity upon the problems that as a fact interested him. He knew that he loved these problems because of their intense human interest. He knew, then, that he was indeed laboring in the service of mankind. But he so loved what he called the concrete, the particular, the individual, that he naturally made little attempt to define his office in terms of any social organism, or of any such object as our national life, viewed as an entity. And he especially disliked to talk of causes in the abstract, or of social movements as I am here characterizing them. His world seemed to him to be made up of individuals — men, events, experiences, and deeds. And he always very little knew how important he himself was, or what vast inarticulate social forces were finding in him their voice. But we are now viewing James from without, in a way that is of course as imperfect as it is inevitable. We therefore have a right at this point to attribute to him an office that, as I believe, he never attributed to himself.

And here we have to speak first of James's treatment of religious problems, and then of his attitude towards ethics.

Our nation since the civil war has largely lost touch with the older forms of its own religious life. It has been seeking for new embodiments of the religious consciousness, for creeds that shall not be in conflict with the modern man's view of life. It was James's office, as psychologist and as philosopher, to give a novel expression to this our own national variety of the spirit of religious unrest. And his volume, "The Varieties of Religious Experience," is one that, indeed, with all its wealth of illustration, and in its courageous enterprise, has a certain classic beauty. Some men preach new ways of salvation. James simply portrayed the meaning that the old ways of salvation had possessed, or still do possess, in the inner and personal experience of those individuals whom he has called the religious geniuses. And then he undertook to suggest an hypothesis as to what the whole religious process might mean. The hypothesis is on the one hand in touch with certain tendencies of recent psychology. And in so far it seems in harmony with the modern consciousness. On the other hand it expresses, in a way, James's whole philosophy of life. And in this respect it comes into touch with all the central problems of humanity.

The result of this portrayal was indeed magical. The psychologists were aided towards a new tolerance in their study of religion. The evolution of religion appeared in a new light. And meanwhile many of the faithful, who had long been disheartened by the later forms of evolutionary naturalism, took heart anew when they read James's vigorous appeal to the religious experience of the individual as to the most authoritative evidence for religion. "The most modern of thinkers, the evolutionist, the psychologist," they said, "the heir of all the ages, has thus vindicated anew the witness of the spirit in the heart — the very source of inspiration in which we ourselves have always believed." And such readers went away rejoicing, and some of them even began to write christologies based upon the doctrine of James as they understood it. The new gospel, the glad tidings of the subconscious, began to be preached in many lands. It has even received the signal honor of an official papal condemnation.

For my own part, I have ventured to say elsewhere that the new doctrine, viewed in one aspect, seems to leave religion in the comparatively trivial position of a play with whimsical powers — a prey to endless psychological caprices. But James's own robust faith was that the very caprices of the spirit are the opportunity for the building up of the highest forms of the spiritual life; that the unconventional and the individual in religious experience are the means whereby the truth of a superhuman world may become most manifest. And this robust faith of James, I say, whatever you may think of its merits, is as American in type as it has already proved effective in the expression which James gave to it. It is the spirit of the frontiersman, of the gold seeker, or the home builder, transferred to the metaphysical and to the religious realm. There is our far-off home, our long-lost spiritual fortune. Experience alone can guide us towards the place where these things are; hence you indeed need experience. You can only win your way on the frontier in case you are willing to live there. Be, therefore, concrete, be fearless, be experimental. But, above all, let not your abstract conceptions, even if you call them scientific conceptions, pretend to set any limits to the richness of spiritual grace, to the glories of spiritual possession, that, in case you are duly favored, your personal experience may reveal to you. James reckons that the tribulations with which abstract scientific theories have beset our present age are not to be compared with the glory that perchance shall be, if only we open our eyes to what experience itself has to reveal to us.

In the quest for the witness to whom James appeals when he tests his religious doctrine, he indeed searches the most varied literature; and of course most of the records that he consults belong to foreign lands. But the book called "The Varieties of Religious Experience" is full of the spirit that, in our country, has long been effective in the formation of new religious sects; and this volume expresses, better than any sectarian could express, the recent efforts of this spirit to come to an understanding with modern naturalism, and with the new psychology. James's view of religious experience is meanwhile at once deliberately unconventional and intensely democratic. The old-world types of reverence for the external forms of the church find no place in his pages; but equally foreign to his mind is that barren hostility of the typical European freethinkers for the church with whose traditions they have broken. In James's eyes, the forms, the external organizations of the religious world simply wither; it is the individual that is more and more. And James, with a democratic contempt for social appearances, seeks his religious geniuses everywhere. World-renowned saints of the historic church receive his hearty sympathy; but they stand upon an equal footing, in his esteem, with many an obscure and ignorant revivalist, with faith healers, with poets, with sages, with heretics, with men that wander about in all sorts of sheepskins and goatskins, with chance correspondents of his own, with whomsoever you will of whom the world was not and is not worthy, but who, by inner experience, have obtained the substance of things hoped for, the evidence of things not seen.

You see, of course, that I do not believe James's resulting philosophy of religion to be adequate. For as it stands it is indeed chaotic. But I am sure that it can only be amended by taking it up into a larger view, and not by rejecting it. The spirit triumphs, not by destroying the chaos that James describes, but by brooding upon the face of the deep until the light comes, and with light, order. But I am sure also that we shall always have to reckon with James's view. And I am sure also that only an American thinker could have written this survey, with all its unconventional ardor of appreciation, with all its democratic catholicity of sympathy, with all its freedom both from ecclesiastical formality and from barren free-thinking. I am sure also that no book has better expressed the whole spirit of hopeful unrest, of eagerness to be just to the modern view of life, of longing for new experience, which characterizes the recent American religious movement. In James's book, then, the deeper spirit of our national religious life has found its most manifold and characteristic expression.

III

I must next turn to the other of the two aspects of James's work as a thinker that I mentioned above; namely, to his ethical influence. Since the war, our transformed and restless people has been seeking not only for religious, but for moral guidance. What are the principles that can show us the course to follow in the often pathless wilderness of the new democracy? It frequently seems as if, in every crisis of our greater social affairs, we needed somebody to tell us both our dream and the interpretation thereof. We are eager to have life, and that abundantly. But what life? And by what test shall we know the way of life?

The ethical maxims that most readily meet the popular demand for guidance in such a country, and at such a time, are maxims that combine attractive vagueness with an equally winning pungency. They must seem obviously practical; but must not appear excessively rigorous. They must arouse a large enthusiasm for action, without baffling us with the sense of restraint, or of wearisome self-control. They must not call for extended reflection. Despite their vagueness they must not appear abstract, nor yet hard to grasp. The wayfaring man, though a fool, must be sure that he at least will not err in applying our moral law. Moral blunders must be natural only to opponents, not to ourselves. We must be self-confident. Moreover, our moral law must have an athletic sound. Its first office is to make us "good sports." Only upon such a law can we meditate day and night, in case the "game" leaves us indeed any time for meditation at all. Nevertheless, these popular maxims will of course not be meant as mere expressions of blind impulse. On the contrary, they will appeal to highly intelligent minds, but to minds anxious for relief from the responsibility of being too thoughtful. In order to be easily popular they must be maxims that stir the heart, not precisely indeed like the sound of a trumpet, but more like the call of the horn of an automobile. You will have in mind the watchwords that express some of the popular ethical counsels thus suggested. One of these watchwords has of late enabled us to abbreviate a well-known and surely a highly intelligent maxim, to something that is to-day used almost as a mere interjection. It is the watchword, "Efficiency"! Another expression of the same motive takes shape in the equally familiar advice, "Play the game."

Now I do not mean to make light of the real significance of just such moral maxims, for awakening and inspiring just our people in this day. The true value of these maxims lies for us in three of their characteristic features. First, they give us counsel that is in any case opposed to sloth. And sloth on every level of our development remains one of the most treacherous and mortal enemies of the moral will. Secondly, they teach us to avoid the dangers to which the souls of Hamlet's type fall a prey. That is, they discourage the spirit that reflectively divides the inner self, and that leaves it divided. They warn us that the divided self is indeed, unless it can heal its deadly wound, by fitting action, a lost soul. And thirdly, they emphasize courage. And courage, — not, to be sure, so much the courage that faces one's rivals in the market place, or one's foes on the battlefield, as the courage that fits us to meet our true spiritual enemies, — the courage that arises anew from despair and that undertakes, despite all tribulations, to overcome the world — such courage is one of the central treasures of the moral life.

Because of these three features, the maxims to which I refer are, in all their vagueness, vehicles of wisdom. But they express themselves in their most popular forms with a willfulness that is often more or less comic, and that is sometimes tragic. For what they do not emphasize is the significance of self-possession, of lifting up our eyes to the hills whence cometh our help, of testing the life that now is by the vision of the largest life that we can in ideal appreciate. These popular maxims also emphasize results rather than ideals, strength rather than cultivation, temporary success rather than wholeness of life, the greatness of "Him that taketh a city," rather than of "Him that ruleth his spirit." They are the maxims of unrest, of impatience, and of a certain humane and generous unscrupulousness, as fascinating as it is dangerous. They characterize a people that is indeed earnestly determined to find itself, but that so far has not found itself.

Now one of the most momentous problems regarding the influence of James is presented by the question: How did he stand related to these recent ethical tendencies of our nation? I may say at once that, in my opinion, he has just here proved himself to be most of all and in the best sense our national philosopher. For the philosopher must not be an echo. He must interpret. He must know us better than we know ourselves, and this is what indeed James has done for our American moral consciousness. For, first, while he really made very little of the formal office of an ethical teacher and seldom wrote upon technical ethical controversies, he was, as a fact, profoundly ethical in his whole influence. And next, he fully understood, yet shared in a rich measure, the motives to which the ethical maxims just summarized have given expression. Was not he himself restlessly active in his whole temperament? Did he not love individual enterprise and its free expression? Did he not loathe what seemed to him abstractions? Did he not insist that the moralist must be in close touch with concrete life? As psychologist did he not emphasize the fact that the very essence of conscious life lies in its active, yes, in its creative relation to experience? Did he not counsel the strenuous attitude towards our tasks? And are not all these features in harmony with the spirit from which the athletic type of morality just sketched seems to have sprung?

Not only is all this true of James, but, in the popular opinion of the moment, the doctrine called pragmatism, as he expounded it in his Lowell lectures, seems, to many of his foreign critics, and to some of those who think themselves his best followers here at home, a doctrine primarily ethical in its force, while, to some minds, pragmatism seems also to be a sort of philosophical generalization of the efficiency doctrine just mentioned. To be sure, any closer reader of James's "Pragmatism" ought to see that his true interests in the philosophy of life are far deeper than those which the maxims "Be efficient" and "Play the game" mostly emphasize. And, for the rest, the book on pragmatism is explicitly the portrayal of a method of philosophical inquiry, and is only incidentally a discourse upon ethically interesting matters. James himself used to protest vigorously against the readers who ventured to require of the pragmatist, viewed simply as such, any one ethical doctrine whatever. In his book on "Pragmatism" he had expounded, as he often said, a method of philosophizing, a definition of truth, a criterion for interpreting and testing theories. He was not there concerned with ethics. A pragmatist was free to decide moral issues as he chose, so long as he used the pragmatic method in doing so; that is, so long as he tested ethical doctrines by their concrete results, when they were applied to life.

Inevitably, however, the pragmatic doctrine, that both the meaning and the truth of ideas shall be tested by the empirical consequences of these ideas and by the practical results of acting them out in life, has seemed both to many of James's original hearers, and to some of the foreign critics just mentioned, a doctrine that is simply a characteristic Americanism in philosophy —

a tendency to judge all ideals by their practical efficiency, by their visible results, by their so-called "cash values."

James, as I have said, earnestly protested against this cruder interpretation of his teaching. The author of "The Varieties of Religious Experience" and of "The Pluralistic Universe" was indeed an empiricist, a lover of the concrete, and a man who looked forward to the future rather than backward to the past; but despite his own use, in his "pragmatism" of the famous metaphor of the "cash values" of ideas, he was certainly not a thinker who had set his affections upon things below rather than upon things above. And the "consequences" upon which he laid stress when he talked of the pragmatic test for ideas were certainly not the merely worldly consequences of such ideas in the usual sense of the word "worldly." He appealed always to experience; but then for him experience might be, and sometimes was, religious experience — experience of the unseen and of the superhuman. And so James was right in his protest against these critics of his later doctrine. His form of pragmatism was indeed a form of Americanism in philosophy. And he too had his fondness for what he regarded as efficiency, and for those who "play the game," whenever the game was one that he honored. But he also loved too much those who are weak in the eyes of this present world — the religious geniuses, the unpopular inquirers, the noble outcasts. He loved them, I say, too much to be the dupe of the cruder forms of our now popular efficiency doctrine. In order to win James's most enthusiastic support, ideas and men needed to express an intense inner experience along with a certain unpopularity which showed that they deserved sympathy. Too much worldly success, on the part of men or of ideas, easily alienated him. Unworldliness was one of the surest marks, in his eyes, of spiritual power, if only such unworldliness seemed to him to be joined with interests that, using his favorite words, he could call "concrete" and "important."

In the light of such facts, all that he said about judging ideas by their "consequences" must be interpreted, and therefore it is indeed unjust to confound pragmatism with the cruder worship of efficiency.

IV

Yet, I repeat, James's philosophy of life was indeed, in its ethical aspects, an expression of the better spirit of our people. He understood, he shared, and he also transcended the American spirit. And just that is what most marks him as our national philosopher. If you want to estimate his philosophy of life in its best form, you must read or re-read, not the "Pragmatism," but the essays contained in the volume entitled "The Will to Believe."

May I still venture, as I close, to mention a few features of the doctrine that is embodied in that volume? The main question repeatedly considered in these essays of James is explicitly the question of an empiricist, of a man averse to abstractions, and of an essentially democratic thinker, who does not believe that any final formulation of an ideal of human life is possible until the last man has had his experience of life, and has uttered his word. But this empiricism of the author is meanwhile the empiricism of one who especially emphasizes the central importance of the active life as the basis of our interpretation of experience. Herein James differs from all traditional positivists. Experience is never yours merely as it comes to you. Facts are never mere data. They are data to which you respond. Your experience is constantly transformed by your deeds. That this should be the case is determined by the most essential characteristics of your consciousness. James asserts this latter thesis as psychologist, and has behind him, as he writes, the vast mass of evidence that his two psychological volumes present. The simplest perception, the most elaborate scientific theory, illustrate how man never merely finds, but also always coöperates in creating his world.

No doubt then life must be estimated and guided with constant reference to experience, to consequences, to actual accomplishments, to what we Americans now call efficiency. But on the other hand efficiency itself is not to be estimated in terms of mere data. Our estimate of our world is not to be forced upon us by any mere inspection of consequences. What makes life worth living is not what you find in it, but what you are ready to put into it by your ideal interpretation of the meaning that, as you insist, it shall possess for you. This ideal meaning is always for you a matter of faith not to be imposed coercively upon another, but also never to be discovered by watching who it is that wins, or by merely feeling your present worldly strength as a player of the game. Your deeper ideals always depend upon viewing life in the light of larger unities than now appear, upon viewing yourself as a coworker with the universe for the attainment of what no present human game of action can now reveal. For this "radical empiricist" then present experience always points beyond itself to a realm that no human eye has yet seen — an empirical realm of course, but one that you have a right to interpret in terms of a faith that is itself active, but that is not merely worldly and athletic. The philosophy of action thus so imperfectly suggested by the few phrases that I have time to use can best be interpreted, for the moment, by observing that the influence of Carlyle in many passages of this volume is as obvious as it is by our author independently reinterpreted and transformed. Imagine Carlyle transformed into a representative American thinker, trained as a naturalist, deeply versed in psychology, deprived of his disposition to hatred, open-minded towards the interests of all sorts and conditions of men, still a hero worshiper, but one whose heroes could be found in the obscurest lovers of the ideal as easily as in the most renowned historical characters; let this transformed Carlyle preach the doctrine of the resolute spirit triumphant through creative action, defiant of every degree of mortal suffering. Let him proclaim "The Everlasting Yea" in the face of all the doubts of erring human opinion: and herewith you gain some general impression of the relations that exist between "Sartor Resartus" and "The Will to Believe."

The ethical maxims which are scattered through these pages voluntarily share much of the vagueness of our age of tentative ethical effort. But they certainly are not the maxims of an impressionist, of a romanticist, or of a partisan of merely worldly efficiency. They win their way through all such attitudes to something beyond — to a resolute interpretation of human life as an opportunity to coöperate with the superhuman and the divine. And they do this, in the author's opinion, not by destroying, but by fulfilling the purposes and methods of the sciences of experience themselves. Is not every scientific theory a conceptual reinterpretation of our fragmentary perceptions, an active reconstruction, to be tried in the service of a larger life? Is not our trust in a scientific theory itself an act of faith? Moreover, these ethical maxims are here governed, in James's exposition, by the repeated recognition of certain essentially absolute truths, truths that, despite his natural horror of absolutism, he here expounds with a finished dialectic skill that he himself, especially in his later polemic period, never seemed to prize at its full value. The need of active faith in the unseen and the superhuman he founds upon these simple and yet absolutely true principles, principles of the true dialectics of life: First, every great decision of practical life requires faith, and has irrevocable consequences, consequences that belong to the whole great world, and that therefore have endless possible importance. Secondly, since action and belief are thus inseparably bound together, our right to believe depends upon our right, as active beings, to make decisions. Thirdly, our duty to decide life's greater issues is determined by the absolute truth that, in critical cases, the will to be doubtful and not to decide is itself a decision, and is hence no escape from our responsible moral position. And this our responsible position is a position that gives us our place in and for all future life. The world needs our deeds. We need to interpret the world in order to act. We have a right to interpret the universe so as to enable us to act at once decisively, courageously, and with the sense of the inestimable preciousness and responsibility of the power to act.

In consequence of all these features of his ethical doctrine a wonderful sense of the deep seriousness and of the possibly divine significance of every deed is felt in James's every ethical counsel. Thus it is that, while fully comprehending the American spirit which we have sketched, he at once expresses it and transforms it. He never loved Fichte; but there is much of the best of the ethical idealism of Fichte in "The Will to Believe." Many of you have enjoyed James's delightfully skillful polemic against Hegel, and against the external forms, phrases, and appearances of the later constructive idealists. I have no wish here to attempt to comment upon that polemic; but I can assure you that I myself learned a great part of my own form of absolute idealism from the earliest expressions that James gave to the thoughts contained in "The Will to Believe." As one of his latest works, "The Pluralistic Universe," still further showed, he himself was in spirit an ethical idealist to the core. Nor was he nearly so far in spirit even from Hegel as he supposed, guiltless as he was of Hegel's categories. Let a careful reading of "The Pluralistic Universe" make this fact manifest.

Meanwhile, what interests us is that, in "The Will to Believe," as well as in "The Pluralistic Universe," this beautifully manifold, appreciative, and humane mind, at once adequately expressed, and, with true moral idealism, transcended the caprices of recent American ethics. To this end he lavishly used the resources of the naturalist, of the humanist, and of the ethical dialectician. He saw the facts of human life as they are, and he resolutely lived beyond them into the realm of the spirit. He loved the concrete, but he looked above towards the larger realm of universal life. He often made light of the abstract reason, but in his own plastic and active way he uttered some of the great words of the universal reason, and he has helped his people to understand and to put into practice these words.

I ask you to remember him then, not only as the great psychologist, the radical empiricist, the pragmatist, but as the interpreter of the ethical spirit of his time and of his people — the interpreter who has pointed the way beyond the trivialities which he so well understood and transcended towards that "Rule of Reason" which the prophetic maxim of our supreme court has just brought afresh to the attention of our people. That "Rule of Reason," when it comes, will not be a mere collection of abstractions. It will be, as James demanded, something concrete and practical. And it will indeed appeal to our faith as well as to our discursive logical processes. But it will express the transformed and enlightened American spirit as James already began to express it. Let him too be viewed as a prophet of the nation that is to be.

ESSAY II

LOYALTY AND INSIGHT

ESSAY II

LOYALTY AND INSIGHT [1]

UPON an occasion like this, when the children, the servants, and the friends of this institution meet for their annual festival, there is one word that best expresses the spirit of the occasion. It is the word "loyalty," — loyalty to your College, to its ideals, to its life, and to the unity and effectiveness of this life. And amongst the ideals that inspire the life of your College, and make that life effective and united, there is one which is prominent in all your minds, whatever your special studies, your practical aims, or your hopes. It is the ideal of furthering, in all your minds, what we may call insight, — the ideal of learning to see life as it is, to know the world as we men need to know it, and to guide our purposes as we ought to guide them. It is

[1] Commencement Address delivered at Simmons College, Boston, in June, 1910.

LOYALTY AND INSIGHT

also the ideal of teaching to others the art of just such insight.

These two words, then, "loyalty" and "insight," name, one of them, the spirit in which, upon such occasions as this, we all meet; the other, the ideal that determines the studies and the researches of any modern institution of learning. Upon each day of its year of work your College says to its children and to its servants and to its community: "Let us know, let us see, let us comprehend, let us guide life by wisdom, and in turn let us discover new wisdom for the sake of winning new life." But upon a day like the present one, the work of the year being laid aside, your College asks and receives your united expression of loyalty to its cause. Perhaps some of you may feel that for just this moment you have left behind, at least temporarily, the task of winning insight. You enjoy, for the hour, the fruits of toil. Study and research cease, you may say, for to-day, while the spirit of loyalty finds its own free expression and takes content in its holiday.

I agree that the holidays and the working

LOYALTY AND INSIGHT

days have a different place in our lives. But it is my purpose in this address to say something about the connections between the spirit which rules this occasion — the spirit of loyalty — and the ideal by which the year's work has to be guided, — the ideal of furthering true insight. The loyalty that now fills your minds is merely one expression of a certain spirit which ought to pervade all our lives — not only in our studies, but in our homes, in our offices, in our political and civic life — not merely upon holidays, or upon other great occasions, but upon our working days; and most of all when our tasks seem commonplace and heavy. And, on the other hand, the insight which you seek to get whenever, in the academic world, you work in the laboratory or in the field, in the library or in the classroom or alone in your study, the insight that you try both to embody in your practical life and to enrich through your researches, — just this insight, I say, is best to be furthered by a right cultivation of the spirit of loyalty.

LOYALTY AND INSIGHT

I suppose that when I utter these words, you will easily give to them a certain general assent. But I want to devote this address to making just such words mean more to you than at first sight they may appear to mean.

First, then, let me tell you what I myself mean by the term "loyalty." Then let me deal with my principal thesis, which is that the true spirit of loyalty is not merely a proper accompaniment of all serious work, but is an especially important source of a very deep insight into the meaning of life, and, as I personally believe, into the nature of the whole universe.

Three sorts of persons, I have noticed, are fond of using the term "loyalty." These are quite different types of persons; or, in any case, they use the word upon very different occasions. But these very differences are to my mind important. The first type of those who love to use the term "loyalty" consists of those who employ it to express a certain glow of enthusiastic devotion, the type of the lovers, of the students when the

LOYALTY AND INSIGHT

athletic contests are near, of the partisans in the heat of a political contest, or of the friends of an institution upon a day like this. To such persons, or at least at such moments, loyalty is conceived as something brilliantly emotional, as a passion of devotion. The second class of those who are fond of the word "loyalty" are the warriors and their admirers. To such persons loyalty means a willingness to do dangerous service, to sacrifice life, to toil long and hard for the flag that one follows. But for a third type of those who employ the word, loyalty especially means steady, often unobtrusive, fidelity to more or less formal obligations, such as the business world and the workshop impose upon us. Such persons think of loyalty as, first of all, faithfulness in obeying the law of the land, or in executing the plans of one's official superiors, or in serving one's employer or one's client or one's chief, or one's fraternity or other social union. In this sense the loyal servant may be obscure and unemotional. But he is trustworthy. Now, a word which thus so forcibly

LOYALTY AND INSIGHT

appeals to the lovers who want to express their passionate devotion, and also to the soldiers who want to name that obstinate following of the flag which makes victory possible; a word which business men also sometimes use to characterize the quietly and industriously faithful employee who obeys orders, who betrays no secrets, and who regards the firm's interest as his own; — well, such a word, I think, is not as much ambiguous as deep in its meaning. For, after all, loyal emotions, loyal sacrifice of life, loyal steadiness in obscure service, are but various symptoms of a certain spirit which lies beneath all its various expressions. This spirit is a well-known one. All the higher life of society depends upon it. It may manifest itself as enthusiasm upon an occasion like this, or as contempt for death upon the battle field, or as quiet service when the toil of life is grim, or as the cool fidelity that pursues the daily routine of office or of workshop or of kitchen with a steady persistence and with a simple acceptance of traditional duties or of the day's toil. But the spirit thus manifested is not exhausted by any of its symptoms. The appearances of loyalty are manifold. Its meaning is one. And I myself venture to state what the true spirit of loyalty is by defining the term thus: By loyalty I mean the thoroughgoing, the voluntary, and the practical devotion of a self to a cause. And by a cause I mean something of the nature that the true lover has in mind when he is wisely devoted to his love; that the faithful member of a family serves when the family itself is the cause dear to him; that the member of a fraternity, or the child of a college, or the devoted professional man, or the patriot, or the martyr, or the faithful workman conceives when he thinks of that to which he gives his life. As all these illustrations suggest, the cause to which one can be loyal is never a mere detached individual, and never a mere collection of individuals; nor is it ever a mere abstract principle. This cause, whether in the church or the army or the workshop, in the home or in the friendship, is some sort of unity whereby many persons are joined in one common life. The cause to which a loyal man is devoted is of the nature of an institution, or of a home life, or of a fraternity, wherein two or more persons aim to become one; or of a religion, wherein the unity of the spirit is sought through the communion of the faithful. Loyalty respects individuals, but aims to bring them together into one common life. Its command to the loyal is: "Be 'one undivided soul of many a soul.'" It recognizes that, when apart, individuals fail; but that when they try to unite their lives into one common higher selfhood, to live as if they were the expressions, the instruments, the organs of one ideally beautiful social group, they win the only possible fulfillment of the meaning of human existence. Through loyalty to such a cause, through devotion to an ideally united social group, and only through such loyalty, can the problems of human personality be solved. By nature, and apart from some cause to which we are loyal, each of us is but a mass of caprices, a chaos of distracting passions, a longing for happiness that is never fulfilled, a seeking for success which never attains its goal. Meanwhile, no merely customary morality ever adequately guides our lives. Mere social authority never meets our needs. But a cause, some unity of many lives in one, some call upon the individual to give himself over to the service of an idealized community, — this gives sense to life. This, when we feel its presence, as we do upon this occasion, we love, as the lovers love the common life of friendship that is to make them one, or as the mothers delight in the life that is to unite themselves and their children in the family, or as the devout feel that through their communion in the life of their church they become one with the Divine Spirit. For such a cause we can make sacrifices, such as the soldier makes in following the flag. For what is the fortune of any detached self as compared with the one cause of the whole country? And just such a voluntary devotion to a cause can ennoble the routine of the humblest daily business, in the office, in the household, in the school, at the desk, or in the market place, if one only finds the cause that can hold his devotion — be this cause his business firm or his profession or his household or his country or his church, or all these at once. For all these causes have their value in this: that through the business firm, or the household, or the profession, or the spiritual community, the lives of many human selves are woven into one, so that our fortunes and interests are no longer conceived as detached and private, but as a giving of ourselves in order that the social group to which we are devoted should live its own united life.

With this bare indication of what I mean by loyalty, I may now say that of late years I have attempted to show in detail, in various discussions of our topic, that the spirit of loyalty, rightly understood, and practically applied, furnishes an adequate solution for all the problems of the moral life. The whole moral law can be summed up in the two commandments: first, Be loyal; and secondly, So choose, so serve, and so unify the life causes to which you yourself are loyal that, through your choice, through your service, through your example, and through your dealings with all men, you may, as far as in you lies, help other people to be loyal to their own causes; may avoid cheating them of their opportunities for loyalty; may inspire them with their own best type of loyalty; and may so best serve the one great cause of the spread of loyalty amongst mankind. Or, if I may borrow and adapt for a worthy end Lincoln's immortal words, the moral law is this: Let us so live, so love, and so serve that loyalty "of the people, by the people, for the people, shall not perish from the earth," but shall prosper and abound.

The scheme of life thus suggested is, I believe, adequate. I next want to tell what bearing the spirit of loyalty has upon insight.

The insight that all of us most need and desire is an insight, first, into the business of life itself, and next into the nature and meaning of the real world in which we live. Our forefathers used to center all their views of life and of the world about their religion. Many of the leading minds of to-day center their modern insight about the results of science. In consequence, what I may call the general problems of insight, and the views of life and of the world which most of us get from our studies, have come of late to appear very different from the views and the problems which our own leading countrymen a century ago regarded as most important. The result is that the great problem of the philosophy of life to-day may be defined as the effort to see whether, and how, you can cling to a genuinely ideal and spiritual interpretation of your own nature and of your duty, while abandoning superstition, and while keeping in close touch with the results of modern knowledge about man and nature.

Let me briefly indicate what I mean by this problem of a modern philosophy of life. From the modern point of view great stress has been laid upon the fact that man, as we know man, appears to be subject to the laws of the natural world. Modern knowledge makes these laws appear very far-reaching, very rigid, and very much of the type that we call mechanical. We have, therefore, most of us, learned not to expect miraculous interferences with the course of nature as aids in our human conflict with destiny. We have been taught to regard ourselves as the products of a long process of natural evolution. We have come to think that man's control over nature has to take the general form which our industrial arts illustrate, and which our recent contests with disease, such as the wars with tuberculosis and with yellow fever, exemplify. Man, we have been led to say, wins his way only by studying nature and by applying his carefully won empirical knowledge to the guidance of his arts. The business of life — so we have been moved to assert — must therefore be guided simply by an union of plain common sense with the scientific study of nature. The real world, we have been disposed to say, is, on the whole, so far as we can know it, a mechanism. Therefore the best ideal of life involves simply the more or less complete control of this mechanism for useful and humane ends.

Such, I say, is one very commonly accepted result to which modern knowledge seems to have led men. The practical view of life and of its business which expresses this result has been, for many of us, twofold. First, we have been led to this well-known precept: If you want to live wisely, you must, at all events, avoid superstition. That is, you must not try to guide human life by dealing with such supernatural powers, good and evil, as the mythologies of the past used to view as the controlling forces of human destiny. You must take natural laws as you find them. You must believe about the real world simply what you can confirm by the verdict of human experience. You must put no false hopes either in magic arts or in useless appeals to the gods. You must, for instance, fight tuberculosis not by prayer, but by knowing the conditions that produce it and the natural processes that tend to destroy its germs. And so, in general, in order to live well and wisely you must be a naturalist and not a supernaturalist. Or in any case you must conform your common sense not to the imagination that in the past peopled the dream world of humanity with good and evil spirits, but to the carefully won insight that has shown us that our world is one where natural law reigns unyielding, defying equally our magic arts and our prayerful desires for divine aid. But secondly, side by side with this decidedly positive advice, many of us have been brought to accept a practical attitude towards the world which has seemed to us negative and discouraging. This second attitude may be expressed in the sad precept: Hope not to find this world in any universal sense a world of ideal values. Nature is indifferent to values. Values are human, and merely human. Man can indeed give to his own life much of what he calls value, if he uses his natural knowledge for human ends. But when he sets out upon this task, he ought to know that, however sweet and ideal human companionship may be as it exists among men, humanity as a whole must fight its battle with nature and with the universe substantially alone, comfortless except for the comforts that it wins precisely as it builds its houses; namely, by using the mechanisms of nature for its own purposes. The world happens, indeed, to give man some power to control natural conditions. But even this power is due to the very fact that man also is one of nature's products, — a product possessing a certain stability, a certain natural plasticity and docility, a limited range of natural initiative. As a rock may deflect a stream, so man, himself a natural mechanism, may turn the stream of nature's energies into paths that are temporarily useful for human purposes. But from the modern point of view the ancient plaint of the Book of Job remains true, both for the rock and for the man:

> "The waters wear away stones,
> And the hope of frail man thou destroyest."

In the end, our relations to the universe thus seem to remain relations to an essentially foreign power, which cares for our ideals as the stormy sea cares for the boat, and as the bacteria care for the human organism upon which they prey. If we ourselves, as products of nature, are sufficiently strong mechanisms, we may be able to win, while life lasts, many ideal goods. But just so, if the boat is well enough built, it may weather one or another passing storm. If the body is well knit, it may long remain immune to disease. Yet in the end the boat and the human body fail. And in no case, so this view asserts, does the real world essentially care for or help or encourage our ideals. Our ideals are as foreign to the real natural world as the interests of the ship's company are to the ocean that may tolerate, but also may drown them. Be free from superstition, then; and next avoid false hopes. Such are the two theses that seem to embody for many minds the essentially modern view of things and the essential result for the philosophy of life of what we have now learned.

But hereupon the question arises whether

this is indeed the last word of insight; whether this outcome of modern knowledge does indeed tell the whole story of our relations to the real world. That this modern view has its own share of deeper truth we all recognize. But is this the whole truth? Have we no access whatever to any other aspect of reality than the one which this naturalistic view emphasizes? And again, the question still arises: Is there any place left for a religion that can be free from superstition, that can accept just so much of the foregoing modern results as are indeed established, and that can yet supplement them by an insight which may show the universe to be, after all, something more than a mechanism? In sum, are we merely stones that deflect the stream for a while, until the waters wear them away? Or are there spiritual hopes of humanity which the mechanism of nature cannot destroy? Is the philosophy of life capable of giving us something more than a naturalism — humanized merely by the thought that man, being, after all, a well-knit and plastic

LOYALTY AND INSIGHT

mechanism, can for a time mold nature to his ends? So much for the great problem of modern insight. Let us turn to consider the relation of the spirit of loyalty to this problem.

What light can a study of the spirit of loyalty, as I just defined loyalty, — what light, I say, can such a study throw upon this problem? Very little — so some of you may say; for any discussion of the spirit of loyalty can tell us nothing to make nature's mechanism more comprehensible. One who favors loyalty as a way of solving life's problems tells us about a certain ideal of human life, — an ideal which, as I have asserted, does tend to solve our personal moral problems precisely in so far as we are able to express this ideal in our practical lives. In order to be loyal you indeed have no need to believe in any of the well-known miracles of popular tradition. And equally, in order to be loyal, you have no need, first, to decide whether nature is or is not a mechanism; or whether the modern view of reality, as just summarized, is or is not adequate; or whether the gods exist; or whether man is or is not one of nature's products and temporarily well-knit and plastic machines. Our doctrine of loyalty is founded not upon a decision about nature's supposed mechanism, but upon a study of man's own inner and deeper needs. It is a doctrine about the plan and the business of human life. It seems, therefore, to be neutral as to every so-called conflict between science and religion.

But now, in answer to these remarks, I have to show that the doctrine of loyalty, once rightly understood, has yet a further application. It is a doctrine that, when more fully interpreted, helps us toward a genuine insight, not only into the plan of life, but into the nature of things. The philosophy of loyalty has nothing to say against precisely so much of naturalism as is indeed an established result of common sense and of the scientific study of nature. The theory of the loyal life involves nothing superstitious — no trust in magic, no leaning upon the intervention of such spiritual agencies as the old mytholo-

LOYALTY AND INSIGHT

gies conceived. And yet, as I shall insist, nobody can understand and practice the loyal spirit without tending thereby to get a true view of the nature of things, a genuine touch with reality, which cannot be gained without seeing that, however much of a mechanism nature may appear to be, the real world is something much more than a mechanism, and much more significant than are the waters which wear away stones.

Let me indicate what I mean by repeating in brief my doctrine of loyalty — with reference to the spirit which it involves, and with reference to the view of the realities of human life which it inevitably includes.

Whoever is loyal has found some cause, I have said, — a cause to which, by his inner interests, he is indeed attracted, so that the cause is fascinating to his sentiments. But the cause is also one to which the loyal man is meanwhile practically and voluntarily devoted, so that his loyalty is no mere glow of enthusiasm, but is an affair of his deeds as well as of his emotions. Loyalty I therefore defined as the thoroughgoing and practical devotion of a self to a cause. Why loyalty is a duty; how loyalty is possible for every normal human being; how it can appear early in youth, and then grow through life; how it can be at once faithful to its own, and yet can constantly enlarge its scope;, how it can become universally human in its interests without losing its concreteness, and without failing to keep in touch with the personal affections and the private concerns of the loyal person; how loyalty is a virtue for all men, however humble and however exalted they may be; how the loyal service of the tasks of a single possibly narrow life can be viewed as a service of the cause of universal loyalty, and so of the interests of all humanity; how all special duties of life can be stated in terms of a duly generalized spirit of loyalty; and how moral conflicts can be solved, and moral divisions made, in the light of the principle of loyalty; — all this I have asserted, although here is indeed no time for adequate discussion. But hereupon I want to concentrate our whole attention, not upon the consequences and applications of the doctrine of loyalty, but upon the most central characteristic of the loyal spirit. This central characteristic of the loyal spirit consists in the fact that it conceives and values its cause as a reality, as an object that has a being of its own; while the type of reality which belongs to a cause is different from the type of reality which we ascribe either to a thing in the physical world or to a law of nature. A cause is never a mere mechanism. It is an essentially spiritual reality. If the loyal human being is right in the account which he gives of his cause, then the real world contains beings which are not mere natural objects, and is subject to laws which, without in the least running counter to the laws of outer nature, are the laws of an essentially spiritual realm, whose type of being is superior to that possessed by the order of nature which our physical sciences study and which our industrial arts use. Either, then, loyalty is altogether a service of myths, or else the causes which the loyal

LOYALTY AND INSIGHT

serve belong to a realm of real being which is above the level of mere natural fact and natural law. In the latter case the real world is not indifferent to our human search for values. The modern naturalistic and mechanical views of reality are not, indeed, false within their own proper range, but they are inadequate to tell us the whole truth. And reality contains, further, and is characterized by, an essentially spiritual order of being.

I have been speaking to persons who, as I have trusted, well know, so far as they have yet had time to learn the lessons of life, something of what loyalty means. Come, then, let us consider what is the sort of object that you have present to your mind when you are loyal to a cause. If your cause is a reality, what kind of a being is it? If causes are realities, then in what sort of a real world do you live?

I have already indicated that, while loyalty always includes personal affections, while you can never be loyal to what you take to be a merely abstract principle, nevertheless, it is equally true that you can never be genuinely loyal merely to an individual human being, taken just as this detached creature. You can, indeed, love your friend, viewed just as this individual. But love for an individual is so far just a fondness for a fascinating human presence, and is essentially capricious, whether it lasts or is transient. You can be, and should be, loyal to your friendship, to the union of yourself and your friend, to that ideal comradeship which is neither of you alone, and which is not the mere doubleness that consists of you and your friend taken as two detached beings who happen to find one another's presence agreeable. Loyalty to a friendship involves your willingness actively and practically to create and maintain a life which is to be the united life of yourself and your friend — not the life of your friend alone, nor the life of yourself and your friend as you exist apart, but the common life, the life above and inclusive of your distinctions, the one life that you are to live as friends. To the tie, to the unity, to the common life, to the union of friends, you can be loyal. Without such loyalty friendship consists only of its routine of more or less attractive private sentiments and mere meetings, each one of which is one more chance experience, heaped together with other chance experiences. But with such true loyalty your friendship becomes, at least in ideal, a new life, — a life that neither of you could have alone; a life that is not the mere sum of your separate and more or less pleasant private lives; a life that is not a mere round of separate private amusements, but that belongs to a new type of dual yet unified personality. Nor are you loyal to your friendship merely as to an abstraction. You are loyal to it as to the common better self of both of you, a self that lives its own real life. Either such a loyalty to your friendship is a belief in myths, or else such a type of higher and unified dual personality actually possesses a reality of its own, — a reality that you cannot adequately describe by reporting, as to the taker of a census, that you and your friend are two creatures, with two distinct cases of a certain sort of fondness to be noted down, and with each a separate life into which, as an incident, some such fondness enters. No; were a census of true friendship possible, the census taker should be required to report: Here are indeed two friends; but here is also the ideal and yet, in some higher sense, real life of their united personality present, — a life which belongs to neither of them alone, and which also does not exist merely as a parcel of fragments, partly in one, partly in the other of them. It is the life of their common personality. It is a new spiritual person on a higher level.

Or again, you are loyal to some such union as a family or a fraternity represents. Or you are loyal to your class, your college, your community, your country, your church. In all these cases, with endless variety in the details, your loyalty has for its object each time, not merely a group of detached personalities, but some ideally significant common life; an union of many in one; a community which also has the value of a person, and which, nevertheless, cannot be found distributed about in a collection of fragments found inside the detached lives of the individual members of the family, the club, the class, the college, the country, the church. If this common life to which you are loyal is a reality, then the real human world does not consist of separate creatures alone, of the mere persons who flock in the streets and who live in the different houses. The human world, if the loyal are right, contains personality that is not merely shut up within the skin, now of this, now of that, human creature. It contains personalities that no organism confines within its bounds; that no single life, that no crowd of detached lives, comprises. Yet this higher sort of common personality, if the loyal are right, is as real as we separate creatures are real. It is no abstraction. It lives. It loves, and we love it. We enter into it. It is ours, and we belong to it. It works through us, the fellow servants of the common cause. Yet we get our worth through it, — the goal of our whole moral endeavor.

LOYALTY AND INSIGHT

For those who are not merely loyal, but also enlightened, loyalty, never losing the definiteness and the concreteness of its devotion to some near and directly fascinating cause, sees itself to be in actual spiritual unity with the common cause of all the loyal, whoever they are. The great cause for all the loyal is in reality the cause of the spread and the furtherance of the cause of the universal loyalty of all mankind: a cause which nobody can serve except by choosing his own nearer and more immediately appreciated cause, — the private cause which is directly his own, — his family, his community, his friendship, his calling, and the calling of those who serve with him. Yet such personal service — your special life cause, your task, your vocation — is your way of furthering the ends of universal humanity. And if you are enlightened, you know this fact. Through your loyalty you, then, know yourself to be kin to all the loyal. You hereupon conceive the loyal as one brotherhood, one invisible church, for which and in which you live. The spirit dwells in this invisible church, — the holy spirit that wills the unity of all in fidelity and in service. Hidden from you by all the natural estrangements of the present life, this common life of all the loyal, this cause which is the one cause of all the loyal, is that for which you live. In spirit you are really sundered from none of those who themselves live in the spirit.

All this, I say, is what it is the faith of all the loyal to regard as the real life in which we live and move and have our being, precisely in so far as men come to understand what loyalty is. Thus, then, in general, to be loyal is to believe that there are real causes. And to be universally loyal is to believe that the one cause of loyalty itself, the invisible church of all the loyal, is a reality; something as real as we are. But causes are never detached human beings; nor are causes ever mere crowds, heaps, collections, aggregations of human beings. Causes are at once personal (if by person you mean the ordinary human individual in his natural character) and *super-*

LOYALTY AND INSIGHT

personal. Persons they are, because only where persons are found can causes be defined. Superpersonal they are, because no mere individual human creature, and no mere pairs or groups or throngs of human beings, can ever constitute unified causes. You cannot be loyal to a crowd as a crowd. A crowd can shout, as at a game or a political convention. But only some sort of organized unity of social life can either do the work of an unit or hold the effective loyalty of the enlightened worker who does not merely shout with the throng. And so when you are really loyal to your country, your country does not mean to you merely the crowd, the mass of your separate fellow citizens. Still less does it mean the mere organs, or the separate servants of the country, — the customhouse, the War Department, the Speaker of the House, or any other office or official. When you sing "My country, 'tis of thee," you do not mean, "My post office, 'tis of thee," nor yet, "My fellow citizens, 'tis of you, just as the creatures who crowd the street and who overfill the railway cars," that

I sing. If the poet continues in his own song to celebrate the land, the "rocks and rills," the "woods and templed hills," he is still speaking only of symbols. What he means is the country as an invisible but, in his opinion, perfectly real spiritual unity. General Nogi, in a recent Japanese publication about Bushido, expressed his own national ideal beautifully in the words: "Here the sovereign and the people are of one family and have together endured the joys and sorrows of thousands of years." It is that sort of being whereof one speaks when one expresses true loyalty to the country. The country is the spiritual entity that is none of us and all of us, — none of us because it is our unity; all of us because in it we all find our patriotic unity.

Such, then, is the idea that the loyal have of the real nature of the causes which they serve. I repeat, If the loyal are right, then the real world contains other beings than mechanisms and individual human and animal minds. It contains spiritual unities which are as real as we are, but which certainly do not belong to the realm of a mere nature mechanism. Does not all this put the problems of our philosophy of life in a new light?

But I have no doubt that you may at once reply: All this speech about causes is after all merely more or less pleasing metaphor. As a fact, human beings are just individual natural creatures. They throng and struggle for existence, and love and hate and enjoy and sorrow and die. These causes are, after all, mere dreams, or at best entities by courtesy. There are, literally speaking, no such supernatural entities as we have just described. The friends like to talk of being one; but there are always two or more of them, and the unity is a pretty phrase. The country is, in the concrete, the collection of the countrymen, with names, formulas, songs, and so on, attached, by way of poetical license or of convenient abbreviation or of pretty fable. The poet really meant simply that he was fond of the landscape, and was not wholly averse to a good many of his countrymen, and was in any case fond of a good song. Loyalty, like the rest of human life, is an illusion. Nature is real. The unity of the spirit is a fancy.

This, I say, may be your objection. But herewith we indeed stand in the presence of a certain very deep philosophical problem concerning the true definition of what we mean by reality. Into this problem I have neither time nor wish to enter just now. But upon one matter I must, nevertheless, stoutly insist. It is a matter so simple, so significant, so neglected, that I at once need and fear to mention it to you, — need to mention it, because it puts our philosophy into a position that quite transforms the significance of that whole modern view of nature upon which I have been dwelling since the outset of this lecture; fear to mention it, because the fact that it is so commonly neglected shows how hard to be understood it has proved.

That disheartening view of the foreign and mechanical nature of the real world which our sciences and our industrial arts have impressed upon the minds of so many of us; that contempt for superstition; that denial of the supernatural, which seems to the typical modern man the beginning of wisdom; — to what is all this view of reality due? To the results, and, as I believe, to the really important results, of the modern study of natural science. But what is the study of natural science? Practically considered, viewed as one of the great moral activities of mankind, *the study of science is a very beautiful and humane expression of a certain exalted form of loyalty.* Science is, practically considered, the outcome of the absolutely devoted labors of countless seekers for natural truth. But how do we human beings get at what we call natural truth? By observation, — so men say, — and by experience. But by whose experience? By the united, by the synthesized, by the revised, corrected, rationally criticized, above all by the common, experience of many individuals. The possibility of science rests upon the fact that human experience may be progressively treated so as to become more and more an unity. The detached individual records the transit of a star, observes a precipitate in a test tube, stains a preparation and examines it under a microscope, collects in the field, takes notes in a hospital — and loyally contributes his little fragment of a report to the ideally unified and constantly growing totality called scientific human experience. In doing this he employs his memory, and so conceives his own personal life as an unity. But equally he aims — and herein consists his scientific loyalty — to bring his personal experience into unity with the whole course of human experience in so far as it bears upon his own science. The collection of mere data is never enough. It is in the unity of their interpretation that the achievements of science lie. This unity is conceived in the form of scientific theories; is verified by the comparative and critical conduct of experiments. But in all such work how manifold are the presuppositions which we make when we attempt such unification! Here is no place to enumerate these presuppositions. Some of them you find discussed in the textbooks of the logic of science. Some of them are instinctive, and almost never get discussed at all. But it is here enough to say that we all presuppose *that human experience has, or can by the loyal efforts of truth seekers be made to possess, a real unity, superior in its nature and significance to the nature and significance of any detached observer's experience, more genuinely real than is the mere collection of the experiences of any set of detached observers, however large.* The student of natural science is loyal to the cause of the enlargement of this organized and criticized realm of the common human experience. Unless this unity of human experience is a genuine reality, unless all the workers are living a really common life, unless each man is, potentially at least, in a live spiritual unity with his fellows, science itself is a mere metaphor, its truth is an illusion, its results are myths. For science is conceived as true only by conceiving the experiences of countless observers as the sharing of a common realm of experience. If, as we all believe, the natural sciences do throw a real, if indeed an inadequate, light upon the nature of things, then they do so because no one man's experience is disconnected from the real whole of human experience. They do so because the cause to which the loyal study of science is devoted, the cause of the enlargement of human experience, is a cause that has a supernatural, or, as Professor Münsterberg loves to say, an over-individual, type of reality. Mankind is not a mere collection of detached individuals, or man could possess no knowledge of any unity of scientific truth. If men are really only many, and if they have no such unity of conscious experience as loyalty everywhere presupposes, then the cause of science also is a vain illusion, and we have no unified knowledge of nature, only various private fancies about nature. If we know, however ill, nature's mechanism, we do so because human experience is not merely a collection of detached observations, but forms an actual spiritual unity, whose type is not that of a mechanism, whose connections are ideally significant, whose constitution is essentially

LOYALTY AND INSIGHT

that which the ideal of unified truth requires.

So, then, I insist, the dilemma is upon our hands. Either the sciences constitute a progressive, if imperfect, insight into real truth — and then the cause of the unity of human experience is a real cause that really can be served exactly as the lover means to be loyal to his friendship and the patriot to his country; and then also human life really possesses such unity as the loyal presuppose — or else none of this is so. But then loyalty and science alike deal with metaphors and with myths. In the first case the spiritual unity of the life that we lead is essentially vindicated. Causes such as the loyal serve are real. The cause of science also is real. But in that case an essentially spiritual realm, that of the rational unity of human experience, is real; and possesses a grade both of reality and of worth which is superior to the grade of reality that the phenomena of nature's mechanism exhibit to us. In the other case the sciences whose results are supposed to be discouraging and unspiritual vanish, with all their facts, into the realm of fable, together with the world that all the loyal, including the faithful followers of the sciences, believe to be real.

I have here no time to discuss the paradoxes of a totally skeptical philosophy. It is enough to say that such a total skepticism is, indeed, self-refuting. The only rational view of life depends upon maintaining that what the loyal always regard as a reality, namely, their cause, is, indeed, despite all special illusions of this or of that form of imperfect loyalty, essentially a type of reality which rationally survives all criticisms and underlies all doubts.

> "They reckon ill who leave me out;
> When me they fly, I am the wings."

This is what the genuine object of loyalty, the unity of the spiritual life, always says to us when we examine it in the right spirit. But the one source of our deepest insight into this unity of the spirit which underlies all the varieties, and which leads us upward to itself past all the sunderings and doubts of existence, is the loyal spirit itself. Loyalty asserts: "My cause is real. I know that my cause liveth."

LOYALTY AND INSIGHT

But the cause, however imperfectly interpreted, is always some sort of unity of the spiritual life in which we learn to share whenever we begin to be loyal. The more we grow in loyalty and in insight into the meaning of our loyalty, the more we learn to think of some vast range of the unity of spiritual life as the reality to which all the other realities accessible to us are in one way or another subordinate, so that they express this unity, and show more or less what it means. I believe that a sound critical philosophy justifies the view that the loyal, precisely in so far as they view their cause as real, as a personal, but also as an over-individual, realm of genuine spiritual life, are comprehending, as far as they go, the deepest nature of things.

Religion, in its higher sense, always involves a practical relation to a spiritual world which, in its significance, in its inclusiveness, in its unity, and in its close and comforting touch with our most intense personal concerns, fulfills in a supreme degree the requirements which loyalty makes when it seeks for a worthy cause. One may have a true religion without knowing the reason why it is true. One may also have false religious beliefs. But in any case the affiliation of the spirit of the higher religion with the spirit of loyalty has been manifest, I hope, from the outset of this discussion of loyalty. By religious insight one may very properly mean any significant and true view of an object of religious devotion which can be obtained by any reasonable means.

In speaking of loyalty and insight I have also given an indication of that source of religious insight which I believe to be, after all, the surest, the most accessible, the most universal, and, in its deepest essence, the most rational. The problem of the modern philosophy of life is, we have said, the problem of keeping the spirit of religion, without falling a prey to superstition. At the outset of this lecture I told briefly why, in the modern world, we aim to avoid superstition. The true reason for this aim you now see better than at first I could state that reason. We have learned, and wisely learned, that the great cause of the study of nature by scientific methods is one of the principal special causes to which man can be devoted; for nothing serves more than the pursuit of the sciences serves to bind into unity the actual work of human civilization. To this cause of scientific study we have all learned to be, according to our lights, loyal. But the study of science makes us averse to the belief in magic arts, in supernatural interferences, in special providences. The scientific spirit turns from the legends and the superstitions that in the past have sundered men, have inflamed the religious wars, have filled the realm of imagination with good and evil spirits. Turns from these — to what? To a belief in a merely mechanical reality? To a doctrine that the real world is foreign to our ideals? To an assurance that life is vain?

No; so to view the mission of the study of science is to view that mission falsely. The one great lesson of the triumph of science is the lesson of the vast significance of loyalty

LOYALTY AND INSIGHT

to the cause of science. And this loyalty depends upon acknowledging the reality of a common, a rational, a significant unity of human experience, a genuine cause which men can serve. When the sciences teach us to get rid of superstition, they do this by virtue of a loyalty to the pursuit of truth which is, as a fact, loyalty to the cause of the spiritual unity of mankind: an unity which the students of science conceive in terms of an unity of our human experience of nature, but which, after all, they more or less unconsciously interpret just as all the other loyal souls interpret their causes; namely, as a genuine living reality, a life superior in type to the individual lives which we lead — worthy of devoted service, significant, and not merely an incidental play of a natural mechanism. This unity of human experience reveals to us nature's mechanisms, but is itself no part of the mechanism which it observes.

If, now, we do as our general philosophy of loyalty would require: if we take all our loyalties, in whatever forms they may appear, as more or less enlightened but always practical revelations that there is an unity of spiritual life which is above our present natural level, which is worthy of our devotion, which can give sense to life, and which consists of facts that are just as genuinely real as are the facts and the laws of outer nature, — well, can we not thus see our way towards a religious insight which is free from superstition, which is indifferent to magic and to miracle, which accepts all the laws of nature just in so far as they are indeed known, but which nevertheless stoutly insists: "This world is no mere mechanism; it is full of a spiritual unity that transcends mere nature"?

I believe that we can do this. I believe that what I have merely hinted to you is capable of a much richer development than I have here given to these thoughts. I believe, in brief, that in our loyalties we find our best sources of a genuinely religious insight.

Men have often said, "The true source of religious insight is revelation; for these matters are above the powers of human reason."

LOYALTY AND INSIGHT

Now, I am not here to discuss or to criticize anybody's type of revelation. But this I know, and this the believers in various supposed revelations have often admitted, — that unless the aid of some interior spiritual insight comes to be added to the merely external revelation, one can be left in doubt by all possible signs and wonders whereby the revelation undertakes to give us convincing external evidence. Religious faith, indeed, relates to that which is above us, but it must arise from that which is within us. And any faith which has indeed a worthy religious object is either merely a mystic ecstasy, which must then be judged, if at all, only by its fruits, or else it is a loyalty, which never exists without seeking to bear fruit in works. Now my thesis is that loyalty is essentially adoration with service, and that there is no true adoration without practical loyalty. If I am right, all of the loyal are grasping in their own ways, and according to their lights, some form and degree of religious truth. They have won religious insight; for they view something, at least, of the genuine spiritual world in its real unity, and they devote themselves to that unity, to its enlargement and enrichment. And therefore they approach more and more to the comprehension of that true spiritual life whereof, as I suppose, the real world essentially consists.

Therefore I find in the growth of the spirit of loyalty which normally belongs to any loyal life the deepest source of a genuinely significant religious insight which belongs to just that individual in just his stage of development.

In brief: Be loyal; grow in loyalty. Therein lies the source of a religious insight free from superstition. Therein also lies the solution of the problems of the philosophy of life.

ESSAY III

WHAT IS VITAL IN CHISTIANITY?

ESSAY III

WHAT IS VITAL IN CHRISTIANITY?[1]

I DO not venture to meet this company as one qualified to preach, nor yet as an authority in matters which are technically theological. My contribution is intended to present some thoughts that have interested me as a student of philosophy. I hope that one or another of these thoughts may aid others in formulating their own opinions, and in defining their own religious interests, whether these interests and opinions are or are not in agreement with mine.

My treatment of the question, What is vital in Christianity? will involve a study of three different special questions, which I propose to discuss in order, as follows:

1. What sort of faith or of practice is it that can be called vital to any religion?

[1] Prepared for a series of addresses to the Young Men's Christian Association of Harvard University in 1909.

WHAT IS VITAL IN CHRISTIANITY?

That is, By what criteria, in the case of any religion, can that which is vital be distinguished from that which is not vital?

2. In the light of the criteria established by answering this first question, what are to be distinguished as the vital elements of Christianity?

3. What permanent value, and in particular what value for us to-day, have those ideas and practices and religious attitudes which we should hold to be vital for Christianity?

I

The term "vital," as here used, obviously involves a certain metaphor. That is vital for a living organism without which that organism cannot live. So breathing is a vital affair for us all. That is vital for an organic type which is so characteristic of that type that, were such vital features changed, the type in question, if not altogether destroyed, would be changed into what is essentially another type. Thus the contrast between gill breathing and lung breathing appears to be vital for the organic types in question. When we treat the social and mental life which is characteristic of a religion as if it were the life of an organism, or of a type or group of organisms, we use the word "vital" in accordance with the analogies thus indicated.

If, with such a meaning of the word "vital," we turn to the religions that exist among men, we find that any religion presents itself to an observer as a more or less connected group: (1) of religious practices, such as prayers, ceremonies, festivals, rituals, and other observances, and (2) of religious ideas, the ideas taking the form of traditions, legends, and beliefs about the gods or about spirits. On the higher levels, the religious ideas are embodied in sacred books, and some of them are emphasized in formal professions of faith. They also come, upon these higher levels, into a certain union with other factors of spiritual life which we are hereafter to discuss.

Our first question is, naturally, What is the more vital about a religion: its religious practices, or its religious ideas, beliefs, and spiritual attitudes?

As soon as we attempt to answer this question, our procedure is somewhat different, according as we dwell upon the simpler and more primitive, or on the other hand upon the higher and more reflective and differentiated forms or aspects of religion.

In primitive religions, and in the religious lives of many of the more simple-minded and less reflective people of almost any faith, however civilized, the religious practices seem in general to be more important, and more vital for the whole structure of the religious life, than are the conscious beliefs which accompany the practices. I say this is true of primitive religions in general. It is also true for many of the simple-minded followers, even of very lofty religions. This rule is well known to the students of the history of religion in our day, and can easily be illustrated from some of the most familiar aspects of religious life. But it is a rule which, as I frankly confess, has frequently been ignored or misunderstood by philosophers, as well as by others who have been led to approach religions for the sake of studying the opinions of those who hold them. In various religious ideas people may be very far apart, at the same moment when their religious practices are in close harmony. In the world at large, including both the civilized and the uncivilized, we may say that the followers of a cult are, in general, people who accept as binding the practices of that cult. But the followers of the same cult may accompany the acceptance of the cult with decidedly different interpretations of the reason why these practices are required of them, and of the supernatural world which is supposed to be interested in the practices.

In primitive religions this rule is exemplified by facts which many anthropologists have expressed by saying that, on the whole, in the order of evolution, religious practices normally precede at least the more definite religious beliefs. Men come to believe as they do regarding the nature of some supernatural being, largely in consequence of the fact that they have first come to follow some course of conduct, not for any conscious reason at all, but merely from some instinctive tendency which by accident has determined this or that special expression. When the men come to observe this custom of theirs, and to consider why they act thus, some special religious belief often arises as a sort of secondary explanation of their practice. And this belief may vary without essentially altering either the practice or the religion. The pigeons in our college yard cluster about the benevolent student or visitor who feeds them. This clustering is the result of instinct and of their training in seeking food. The pigeons presumably have no conscious ideas or theories about the true nature of the man who feeds them. Of course, they are somehow aware of his presence, and of what he does, but they surely have only the most rudimentary and indefinite germs of ideas about what he is. But if the pigeons were to come to consciousness somewhat after the fashion of primitive men, very probably they would regard this way of getting food as a sort of religious function and would begin to worship the visitor as a kind of god. If they did so, what idea about this god would be to them vital? Would their beliefs show that they first reasoned abstractly from effect to cause, and said, "He must be a being both powerful and benevolent, for otherwise his feeding of us in this way could not be explained"? Of course, if the pigeons developed into theologians or philosophers, they might reason thus. But if they came to self-consciousness as primitive men generally do, they would more probably say at first: "Behold, do we not cluster about him and beg from him, and coo to him; and do we not get our food by doing thus? He is, then, a being whom it is essentially worth while to treat in this way. He responds to our cooing and our clustering. Thus we compel him to feed us. Therefore he is a worshipful being. And this is what we mean by a god; namely, some one whom it is practically useful to conciliate and compel by such forms of worship as we practice."

If one passes from this feigned instance to the facts of early religious life, one easily observes illustrations of a similar process, both in children and in the more primitive religions of men. A child may be taught to say his prayers. His early ideas of God as a giver of good things, or as a being to be propitiated, are then likely to be secondary to such behavior. The prayers he often says long before he sees why. His elders, at least when they follow the older traditions of religious instruction, begin by requiring of him the practice of saying prayers; and then they gradually initiate the child into the ruling ideas of what the practice means. But for such a stage of religious consciousness the prayer is more vital than the interpretation. In primitive religions taboo and ritual alike precede, at least in many cases, those explanations of the taboos and of the ritual practices which inquirers get in answer to questions about the present beliefs of the people con-

WHAT IS VITAL IN CHRISTIANITY?

cerned. As religion grows, practices easily pass over from one religion to another, and through every such transition seem to preserve, or even to increase, their sacredness; but they get in the end, in each new religion into which they enter, a new explanation in terms of opinions, themselves producing, so to speak, the new ideas required to fit them to each change of setting. In this process the practices taken over may come to seem vital to the people concerned, as the Mass does to Catholics. But the custom may have preceded the idea. The Christmas and Easter festivals are well-known and classic examples of this process. Christianity did not initiate them. It assimilated them. But it then explained why it did so by saying that it was celebrating the birth and resurrection of Christ.

It is no part of my task to develop at length a general theory about this frequent primacy of religious practice over the definite formulation of religious belief. The illustrations of the process are, however, numerous. Even on the higher levels of religious development, where the inner life comes to be emphasized, the matter indeed becomes highly complicated; but still, wherever there is an established church, the term "dissenter" often means in popular use a person who will not attend this church, or who will not conform to its practices, much more consciously and decidedly than it means a person whose private ideas about religious topics differ from those of the people with whom he is willing to worship, or whose rules he is willing to obey.

Nevertheless, upon these higher levels a part of the religious requirement very generally comes to be a demand for some sort of orthodoxy. And therefore, upon this level, conformity of practice is indeed no longer enough. However the simple-minded emphasize practice, the religious body itself requires not only the right practice, but also the acceptance of a profession of faith. And on this higher level, and in the opinion of those concerned with the higher aspect of their religion, this acceptance must now be not only a formal act but a sincere one. Here, then, in the life of the higher religions, belief tends to come into a position of primacy which results in a very notable contrast between the higher and the simpler forms and aspects of religious life. When religions take these higher forms, belief is at least officially emphasized as quite equivalent in importance to practice. For those who view matters thus, "He that believeth not shall be damned," an unbeliever is, as such, a foe of the religion in question, and of its gods and of its worshipers. As an infidel he is a miscreant, an enemy not only of the true faith but perhaps of mankind. In consequence, religious persecution and religious wars may come to seem, at least for a time, inevitable means of defending the faith. And those who outgrow, or who never pass through, this stage of warlike propaganda and of persecution may still insist that for them it is faith rather than practice which is the vital element of their religion. To what heights such a view of the religious life may attain, the Pauline epistles bear witness, "Through grace are ye saved." And grace comes by faith, or in the form of faith.

II

So far, then, we have two great phases or stages of religious life. On the one stage it is religious practice; as such, that is for the people concerned the more vital thing. Their belief is relatively secondary to their practice, and may considerably vary, while the practice remains the unvarying, and, for them, vital feature. On the other, and no doubt higher, because more self-conscious, stage it is faith that assumes the conscious primacy. And on this second stage, if you believe not rightly, you have no part in the religion in question. That these two stages or phases of the life of religion are in practice closely intermingled, everybody knows. The primitive and the lofty are, in the religious life of civilized men, very near together. The resulting entanglements furnish endlessly numerous problems for the religious life. For in all the higher faiths those who emphasize the inner life make much of faith as a personal disposition. And this emphasis, contending as it does with the more primitive and simple-minded tendency to lay stress upon the primacy of religious practice, has often led to revolt against existing formalism, against ritual requirements, and so to reforms, to heresies, to sects, or to new world religions. Christianity itself, viewed as a world religion, was the outgrowth of an emphasis upon a certain faith, to which its new practices were to be, and were, secondary. On the other hand, the appeal that every religion makes to the masses of mankind is most readily interpreted in terms of practice. Thus the baptism of a whole tribe or nation, at the command of their chief, has been sometimes accounted conversion. A formal profession of a creed in such cases has indeed become an essential part of the requirements of the religion in question. But this profession itself can be regarded, and often is regarded by whole masses of the people concerned, as a ceremony to be performed obediently, and no doubt willingly, rather than as an expression of any highly conscious inner conviction. In consequence, an individual worshiper may come to repeat the creed as a more or less magic charm, to ward off the demons who are known not to like to hear it; or, again, the individual may rise and say the creed simply because the whole congregation at a certain point of the service has to do so.

In particular, since the creeds of the higher faiths relate to what are regarded as mysteries, while the creed must be repeated by all the faithful, the required belief in the creed is often not understood to imply any clear or wise or even intelligent ideas about what the creed really intends to teach. Even in emphasizing belief, then, one may thus interpret it mainly in terms of a willing obedience. The savage converted to the Roman Catholic Church is indeed taught not only to obey, but to profess belief, and as far as possible to get some sort of genuine inner belief. But he is regularly told that for his imperfect stage of insight it is enough if he is fully ready to say, "I believe what the church believes, both as far as I understand what the church believes and also as far as I do not understand what the church believes." And it is in this spirit that he must repeat the creed of the church. But his ideas about God and the world may meanwhile be as crude as his ignorance determines. He is still viewed as a Christian, if he is minded to accept the God of the church of the Christians, even though he still thinks of God as sometimes a visible and "magnified and non-natural" man, a corporeal presence sitting in the heavens, while the scholastic theologian who has converted him thinks of God as wholly incorporeal, as not situated *in loco* at all, as not even existent in time, but only in eternity, and as spiritual substance, whose nature, whose perfection, whose omniscience, and so on, are the topics of most elaborate definition.

Thus, even when faith in a creed becomes an essential part of the requirements of a religion, one often meets, upon a much higher level, that primacy of the practical over the theoretical side of religion which the child's prayers, and the transplanted festivals, and the conceivable religion of the pigeons illustrate. The faithful convert and his scholastic teacher agree much more in religious practices than in conscious religious ideas.

Meanwhile this very situation itself is regarded by all concerned as by no means satisfactory. And those followers of the higher faiths who take the inner life more seriously are never content with this acceptance of what seems to them merely external formalism. For them faith, whether it is accompanied with a clear understanding or not, means something essentially interior and deep and soul-transforming. Hence they continually insist that no one can satisfy God who does not rightly view God. And thus the conflict between the primacy of the practical and of the right faith constantly tends to assume new forms in the life of all the higher religions. The conflict concerns the question whether right practice or right belief is the more vital confound true faith with the power to formulate the mysteries of the faith, except in so far, indeed, as one trustingly accepts whatever one can understand of the teachings of the church? It is indeed, you will insist, grace that saves, and through faith. But the saving faith, you will continue, is, at least in the present life, nothing theoretical. It is itself a gift of God. And it is essentially a spiritual attitude, — at once practical and such as to involve whatever grade of true knowledge is suited to the present stage of the soul in question. Herein, as some of you will say, the most enlightened and the most pious teachers of various religions, and certainly of very various forms of Christianity, are agreed. What is vital in the highest religion is neither the mere practice as external, nor the mere opinion as an internal formulation. It is the union of the two. It is the reaction of the whole spirit in the presence of an experience of the highest realities of human life and of the universe.

If any of you at this point assert this to be

the solution of the problem as to what is vital in religion, if you insist that such spiritual gifts as the Pauline charity, and such emotional experiences as those of conversion, and of the ascent of the soul to God in prayer, and such moral sincerity as is the soul of all good works, are regarded by our best teachers as the really vital elements in religion, — you are insisting upon a solution of our problem which indeed belongs to a third, and no doubt to a very lofty phase of the religious consciousness. And it is just this third phase or level of the religious consciousness that I am to try to study in these conferences. But were such a statement in itself enough to show every one of us precisely what this vital feature of the higher religions is, and just how it can be secured by every man, and just how our modern world, with all its doubts and its problems, is related to the solution just proposed, I should indeed have no task in these lectures but to repeat the well-known formula, to apply it briefly to the case of Christianity, and to leave the rest to your own personal experience.

IV

But as a fact, and as most of you know by personal experience, the well-known proposal of a solution thus stated is to most of us rather the formulation of a new problem than the end of the whole matter. If this higher unity of faith and practice, of grace and right-mindedness, of the right conduct and the clear insight, of the knowledge of what is real and the feeling for the deepest values of life, — if all this is indeed the goal of the highest religions, and if it constitutes what their best teachers regard as vital, how far are many of us at the present day from seeing our way towards adapting any such solution to our own cases! For us, the modern world is full of suggestions of doubt regarding the articles of the traditional creeds. The moral problems of our time, full of new perplexities, confuse us with regard to what ought to be done. Our spiritual life is too complex to be any longer easily unified, or to be unified merely in the ways useful for earlier generations. Our individualism is too highly conscious to be easily won over to a mood of absorption in any one universal ideal. Our sciences are too complicated to make it easy for us to conceive the world either as a unity or as spiritual. The church is, for most of us, no longer one visible institution with a single authoritative constitution, but a variety of social organizations, each with its own traditions and values. The spirit of Christianity, which even at the outset Paul found so hard to formulate and to reduce to unity, can no longer be formulated by us precisely in his terms. Hence, some of us seek for some still simpler, because more primitive, type of Christianity. But when we look behind Paul for the genuinely primitive Christianity, we meet with further problems, one or two of which we are soon to formulate more precisely in this discussion. In brief, however vital for a religion may be its power to unify the whole man, outer and inner, practical and intellectual, ignorant and wise, emotional and critical, the situation of our time is such that this unification is no longer so presented to us by any one body of religious teaching, that we can simply accept it from tradition (since in the modern world we must both act and think as individuals for ourselves), nor that we can easily learn it from our own experience, since in these days our experience is no longer as full of the religiously inspiring elements as was the experience of the times of Jonathan Edwards, or of the Reformation, or of the founders of the great mediæval religious orders, or of the early Christian church. If this unity of the spiritual life is to be reconquered, we must indeed take account of the old solutions, but we must give to them new forms, and adopt new ways, suited to the ideas and to the whole spirit of the modern world. Hence the proposed solution that I just rehearsed is simply the statement of the common program of all the highest religions of humanity. But how to interpret this program in terms which will make it of live and permanent meaning for the modern world,— this is precisely the religious problem of to-day.

WHAT IS VITAL IN CHRISTIANITY?

To sum up, then, our answer to the first of my three problems; namely, What form of faith or of practice can be called vital to any religion? I reply: In the case of any one of the more primitive religions it is, in general, the religious practices that are the most vital features of that religion; and these practices, in general, are vital in proportion as they are necessary to the social life of the tribe or nation amongst which they flourish, so that, when these vital practices die out, the nation in question either dwindles, or is conquered, or passes over into some new form of social order. Secondly, in the higher religions, because of the emphasis that they lay upon the inner life, and especially in the world religions, such as Buddhism, Mohammedanism, and Christianity, belief tends to become a more and more vital feature of the religions in question, and the beliefs — such as monotheism, or the acceptance of a prophet, or of a longer or shorter formulated creed — are vital to such a religion in ways and to degrees which the preachers and the missionaries, the religious wars and the sectarian conflicts of these faiths illustrate, — vital in proportion as the men concerned are ready to labor or to die for these beliefs, or to impose them upon other men, or to insist that no one shall be admitted to the religious community who does not accept them.

But thirdly, as soon as religious beliefs are thus emphasized as over against religious practices, the religious practices are not, thereby, in general set aside or even discouraged. On the contrary, they generally grow more numerous, and often more imposing. And consequently, in the minds of the more ignorant, or of the less earnest, of the faithful there appears throughout the life of these higher religions a constant tendency to revert to the more primitive type of religion, or else never, in fact, to rise above that type. Hence, even in the religions wherein conformity is understood to imply a sincere orthodoxy, the primacy of ritual or of other practice over against faith and the inner life constantly tends to hold its own. There arises in such religions the well-known conflict of inner and outer, of faith and merely external works. This conflict remains a constant source of transformations, of heresies, and of reforms, in all these higher religions, and is in fact an irrepressible conflict so long as human nature is what it is. For a great mass of the so-called faithful, it is the conformity of practice that thus remains vital. But the teachers of the religion assert that the faith is vital.

And now, fourthly, the higher religions, especially as represented in their highest type of teachings, are deeply concerned in overcoming and in reducing to unity this conflict of formal observance with genuine faith, wherever the conflict arises. The proposed solution which is most familiar, most promising, if it can be won, and most difficult to be won, is the solution which consists in asserting and in showing, if possible, in life, that what is most vital to religion is not practice apart from faith, nor faith apart from practice, but a complete spiritual reaction of the entire man, — a reaction which, if possible, shall unite a right belief in the unseen world of the faith with the inner perfection and blessedness that ought to result from the indwelling of the truth in the soul, and with that power to do good works and to conform to the external religious requirements which is to be expected from one whose soul is at peace and lives in the light. In a word, what this solution supposes to be most vital to the highest religion is the union of faith and works through a completed spirituality.

Meanwhile, as we have also seen, just our age is especially beset with the problem: How can such a solution be any longer an object of reasonable hope, when the faiths have become uncertain, the practices largely antiquated, our life and our duty so problematic, and our environment so uninspiring to our religious interests? So much, then, for the first of our three problems.

V

It is now our task to consider the second of our questions. How does this problem regarding what is vital to a religion appear when we turn to the special case of Christianity?

Our review of the sorts of elements which are found vital upon the various levels of the religious consciousness will have prepared you to look at once for what is most vital about Christianity upon the third and highest of the three levels that I have enumerated. It is true that in the minds of great masses of the less enlightened and less devoted population of the Christian world certain religious practices have always been regarded as constituting the most vital features of their religion. These practices are especially those which for the people in question imply the obedient acceptance of the sacraments of the church. Of course for such, faith is indeed a condition for the efficacy of the sacraments. But faith expresses itself especially through and in one's relation to these sacraments. Such emphasis upon religious practices is inevitable, so long as human nature is what it is. But Christianity is obviously, upon all of its higher levels, essentially a religion of the inner life; and for all those in any body of Christians who are either more devout or more enlightened the problem of the church has always included, along with other things, the problem of finding and formulating the true faith; and such faith is, to such people, vital to their religion. In consequence of its vast successes in conquering, after a fashion, its own regions of the world, Christianity has had to undertake upon a very large scale, and over a long series of centuries, the task of adapting itself to the needs of peoples who were in very various, and often in very primitive, conditions of culture. Hence, in formulating its faith and practice, it has had full experience of the conflict between those who in a relatively childlike and primitive way regard religious practice as the primal evidence and expression of the possession of the true religion, and those who, on the contrary, insist primarily upon right belief and a rightly guided inner life as a necessary condition for such conduct as can be pleasing to God. Where, as in the case of the Roman Catholic Church, the effort to reconcile these two motives has the longest traditional expression, that is, where the most elaborate official definition of the saving faith has been deliberately joined with the most precise requirements regarding religious practice, the conflict of motives here in question has been only the more notable as a factor in the history of the church, — however completely for an individual believer this very conflict may appear to have been solved. In the Catholic doctrine of the sacraments, in the theory of the conditions upon which their validity depends, and of their effects upon the process of salvation, the most primitive of religious tendencies stand side by side with the loftiest spiritual interests in glaring contrast. On the one hand the doctrine of the sacraments appeals to primitive tendencies, because certain purely magical influences and incantations are in question. The repetition of certain formulas and deeds acts as an irresistible miraculous charm. On the other hand the life of the spirit is furthered through the administration of these same sacraments by some of the deepest and most spiritual of influences, and by some of the most elevated forms of inner life which the consciousness of man has ever conceived. That there is an actual conflict of motives involved in this union of primitive magic with spiritual cultivation, the church in question has repeatedly found, when the greater schisms relating to the validity or to the interpretation of her sacraments have rent the unity of her body, and when, sometimes within her own fold, the mystics have quarreled with the formalists, and both with the modernists, of any period in which the religious life of the church was at all intense.

Most of you will agree, I suppose, as to the sort of solution of such conflicts between the higher and lower aspects of Christianity which is to be sought, in case there is to be any hope of a solution. You will probably be disposed to say: What is vital in Christianity, if Christianity is permanently to retain its vitality at all in our modern world, must be defined primarily neither in terms of mere religious practice nor yet in terms of merely intellectual formulation, but in terms of that unity of will and intellect that may be expressed in the spiritual disposition of the whole man. You will say, What is vital in Christianity must be, if anything, the Christian interpretation of human life, and the life lived in the light of this interpretation. Such a life, you will insist, can never be identified by its formal religious practices, however important, or even indispensable, some of you may believe this or that religious practice to be. Nor can one reduce what is vital in Christianity merely to a formulated set of opinions, since, as the well-known word has it, the devils also believe, and tremble, and, as some of you may be disposed benevolently to add, the philosophers also believe, and lecture. No, you will say, the Christian life includes practices, which may need to be visible and formal; it includes beliefs, which may have to be discussed and formulated; but Christianity is, first of all, an interpretation of life, — an interpretation that is nothing if not practical, and also nothing if not guided from within by a deep spiritual interest and a genuine religious experience.

So far we shall find it easy to agree regarding the principles of our inquiry. Yet, as the foregoing review of the historical conflicts of religion has shown us, we thus merely formulate our problem. We stand at the outset of what we want to do.

What is that interpretation of life which is vital to Christianity? How must a Christian undertake to solve his problem of his own personal salvation? How shall he view the problem of the salvation of mankind? What is that spiritual attitude which is essential to the Christian religion? Thus our second problem now formulates itself.

VI

Amongst the countless efforts to answer these questions there are two which in these discussions we especially need to face. The two answers thus proposed differ decidedly from each other. Each is capable of leading various further and more special formulations of opinion about the contents of the Christian religion.

The first answer may be stated as follows: What is vital about Christianity is simply the spiritual attitude and the doctrine of Christ, as he himself taught this doctrine and this attitude in the body of his authentic sayings and parables, and as he lived all this out in his own life. All in Christianity that goes beyond this — all that came to the consciousness of the church after Christ's own teaching had been uttered and finished — either is simply a paraphrase, an explanation, or an application of the original doctrine of Christ, or else is not vital, — is more or less unessential, mythical, or at the very least external. Grasp the spirit of Christ's own teaching, interpret life as he interpreted it, and live out this interpretation of life as completely as you can, imitating him — and then you are in essence a Christian. Fail to comprehend the spirit of Christ, or to live out his interpretation of life, and you in so far fail to possess what is vital about Christianity. This, I say, is the first of the two answers that we must consider. It is an answer well known to most of you, and an emphasis upon this answer characterizes some of the most important religious movements of our own time.

The second answer is as follows: What is vital about Christianity depends upon regarding the mission and the life of Christ as an organic part of a divine plan for the redemption and salvation of man. While the doctrine of Christ, as his sayings record this doctrine, is indeed an essential part of this mission, one cannot rightly understand, above all one cannot apply, the teachings of Christ, one cannot live out the Christian interpretation of life, unless one first learns to view the person of Christ in its true relation to God, and the work of Christ as an entirely unique revelation and expression of God's will. The work of Christ, however, culminated in his death. Hence, as the historic church has always maintained, it is the cross of Christ that is the symbol of whatever is most vital about Christianity. As for the person of Christ as his life revealed it, — what is vital in Christianity depends upon conceiving this personality in essentially superhuman terms. The prologue to the Fourth Gospel deliberately undertakes to state what for the author of that Gospel is vital in Christianity. This prologue does so by means of the familiar doctrine of the eternal Word that was the beginning, that was with God and was God, and that in Christ was made flesh and dwelt amongst men. Abandon this doctrine, and you give up what is vital in Christianity. Moreover, the work of Christ was essential to the whole relation of his own teachings to the life of men. Human nature being what it is, the teaching that Christ's sayings record cannot enter into the genuine life of any one who has not first been transformed into a new man by means of an essentially superhuman and divine power of grace. It was the work of Christ to open the way whereby this divine grace became and still becomes efficacious. The needed transformation of human nature, the change of life which according to Christ's sayings is necessary as a condition for entering the kingdom of heaven, this is made possible through the effects of the life and death of Christ. This life and death were events whereby man's redemption was made possible, whereby the atonement for sin was accomplished. In brief, what is vital to Christianity includes an acceptance of the two cardinal doctrines of the incarnation and the atonement. For only in case these doctrines are accepted is it possible to interpret life in the essentially Christian way, and to live out this interpretation.

Here are two distinct and, on the whole, opposed answers to the question, What is vital in Christianity? I hope that you will see that each of these answers is an effort to rise above the levels wherein either religious practice or intellectual belief is overemphasized. It is useless for the partisan of the Christianity of the prologue to the Fourth Gospel to accuse his modern opponent of a willingness to degrade Christ to the level of a mere teacher of morals, and Christianity to a mere practice of good works. It is equally useless for one who insists upon the sufficiency of the gospel of Christ simply as Christ's recorded sayings teach it to accuse his opponent of an intention to make true religion wholly dependent upon the acceptance of certain metaphysical opinions regarding the superhuman nature of Christ. No, the opposition between these two views regarding what is vital in Christianity is an opposition that appears on the highest levels of the religious consciousness. It is not that one view says: "Christ taught these and these moral doctrines, and the practice of these teachings constitutes all that is vital in Christianity." It is not that the opposing view says: "Christ was the eternal Word made flesh, and a mere belief in this fact and in the doctrine of the atoning death is the vital feature of Christianity." No, both of these two views attempt to be views upon the third level of the religious consciousness, — views about the whole interpretation of the higher life, and of its relation to God and to the salvation of man. So far, neither view, as its leading defenders now hold it, can accuse the other of lapsing into those more primitive views of religion which I have summarized in the earlier part of this paper. And I have dwelt so long upon a preliminary view of the relations between faith and practice in the history of religion, because I wanted to clear the way for a study of our problem on its genuinely highest level, so that we shall henceforth be clear of certain old and uninspiring devices of controversy. Both parties are really trying to express what is vital in the Christian conception of life. Both view Christianity as a faith which gives sense to life, and also as a mode of life which is centered about a faith. The true dispute arises upon the highest levels. The question is simply this: Is the Gospel which Christ preached, that is, the teaching recorded in the authentic sayings and parables, intelligible, acceptable, vital, in case you take it by itself? Or, does Christianity lose its vitality in case you cannot give a true sense to those doctrines of the incarnation and the to atonement which the traditional Christian world has so long held and so deeply loved? And furthermore, can you, in the light of modern insight, give any longer a reasonable sense to the traditional doctrines of the atonement and the incarnation? In other words: Is Christianity essentially a religion of redemption in the sense in which tradition defined redemption? Or is Christianity simply that religion of the love of God and the love of man which the sayings and the parables so richly illustrate?

However much, upon its lower levels, Christianity may have used and included the motives of primitive religion, this our present question is not reducible to the terms of the relatively lower conflict between a religion of creed and a religion of practice. The issue now defined concerns the highest interests of religious life.

In favor of the traditional view that the essence of Christianity consists, first, in the doctrine of the superhuman person and the redemptive work of Christ, and, secondly, in the interpretative life that rests upon this doctrine, stands the whole authority, such as it is, of the needs and religious experience of the church of Christian history. The church early found, or at least felt, that it could not live at all without thus interpreting the person and work of Christ.

Against such an account of what is vital in Christianity stands to-day for many of us the fact that the doctrine in question seems to be, at least in the main, unknown to the historic Christ, in so far as we can learn what he taught, while both the evidence for the traditional doctrine and the interpretation of it have rested during Christian history upon reports which our whole modern view of the universe disposes many of us to regard as legendary, and upon a theology which many of us can no longer accept as literally true. Whether such objections are finally valid, we must later consider. I mention the objections here because they are familiar, and because in our day they lead many to turn from the tangles of tradition with a thankful joy and relief to the hopeful task of trying to study, to apply, and to live the pure Gospel of Christ as he taught it in that body of sayings which, as many insist, need no legends to make them intelligible, and no metaphysics to make them sacred.

Yet, as a student of philosophy, coming in no partisan spirit, I must insist that this reduction of what is vital in Christianity to the so-called pure Gospel of Christ, as he preached it and as it is recorded in the body of the presumably authentic sayings and parables, is profoundly unsatisfactory. The main argument for doubting that this so-called pure Gospel of Christ contains the whole of what is vital in Christianity rests upon the same considerations that led the historical church to try in its own way to interpret, and hence to supplement, this gospel by reports that may have been indeed full of the legendary, by metaphysical ideas that may indeed have been deeply imperfect, but by a deep instinctive sense of genuine religious values which, after all, was indispensable for later humanity, — a sense of religious values which was a true sense. For one thing, Christ can hardly be supposed to have regarded his most authentically reported religious sayings as containing the whole of his message, or as embodying the whole of his mission. For, if he had so viewed the matter, the Messianic tragedy in which his life work culminated would have been needless and unintelligible. For the rest, the doctrine that he taught is, as it stands, essentially incomplete. It is not a rounded whole. It looks beyond itself for a completion, which the master himself unquestionably conceived in terms of the approaching end of the world, and which the church later conceived in terms of what has become indeed vital for Christianity.

As modern men, then, we stand between opposed views. Each view has to meet hostile arguments. Each can make a case in favor of its value as a statement of the essence of Christianity. On the one hand the Christ of the historically authentic sayings, — whose gospel is, after all, not to be understood except as part of a much vaster religious process;

on the other hand the Christ of legend, whom it is impossible for us modern men longer to conceive as the former ages of the church often conceived him. Can we choose between the two? Which stands for what is vital in Christianity? And, if we succeed in defining this vital element, what can it mean to us to-day, and in the light of our modern world?

Thus we have defined our problems. Our next task is to face them as openly, as truthfully, and as carefully as our opportunity permits.

VII

Let us, then, briefly consider the first of the two views which have been set over against one another.

The teachings of Christ which are preserved to us do indeed form a body of doctrine that one can survey and study without forming any final opinion about the historical character of the narratives with which these teachings are accompanied in the three Synoptic Gospels. The early church preserved the sayings, recorded them, no doubt, in various forms, but learned to regard one or two of the bodies of recorded sayings as especially important and authentic. The documents in which these earliest records were contained are lost to us; but our gospels, especially those of Matthew, Mark, and Luke, preserve the earlier tradition in a way that can be tested by the agreements in the reported sayings as they appear in the different gospels. It is of course true that some of the authentic teachings of Christ concern matters in regard to which other teachers of his own people had already reached insights that tended towards his own. But nobody can doubt that the sayings, taken as a whole, embody a new and profoundly individual teaching, and are what they pretend to be; namely, at least a partial presentation of an interpretation of life, — an interpretation that was deliberately intended by the teacher to revolutionize the hearts and lives of those to whom the sayings were addressed. Since a recorded doctrine, simply taken in itself, and apart from any narrative, is an unquestionable fact, and since a new and individual doctrine is a fact that can be explained only as the work of a person, it is plain that, whatever you think of the narrative portions of the gospels, your estimate of Christ's reported teachings may be freed at once from any of the perplexities that perhaps beset you as to how much you can find out about his life. So much at least he was; namely, the teacher of this doctrine. As to his life, it is indeed important to know that he taught the doctrine as one who fully meant it; that while he taught it he so lived it out as to win the entire confidence of those who were nearest to him; that he was ready to die for it, and for whatever else he believed to be the cause that he served; and that when the time came he did die for his cause. So much of the gospel narrative is with all reasonable certainty to be regarded as historical.

So far, then, one has to regard the teaching of Christ as a perfectly definite object for historical study and personal imitation, and as, in its main outlines, an accessible tradition.

It is impossible to be sure of our tradition as regards each individual saying. But the main body of the doctrine stands before us as a connected whole, and it is in its wholeness that we are interested in comprehending its meaning.

Now there is also no doubt, I have said, that this doctrine is intended as at least a part of an interpretation of life. For the explicit purpose of the teacher is to transform the inner life of his hearers, and thus to bring about, through this transformation, a reform of their individual outer life. It is, furthermore, sure that, while the teaching in question includes a moral ideal, it is no merely moral teaching, but is full of a profoundly religious interest. For the transformation of the inner life which is in question has to do with the whole relation of the individual man to God. And there are especially two main theses of the teacher which do indeed explicitly relate to the realm of the superhuman and divine world, and which therefore do concern what we may call religious metaphysics. That is, these theses are assertions about a reality that does not belong to the physical realm, and that is not confined to the realities which we contemplate when we consider merely ethical truth as such. The first of these religious theses relates to the nature of God. It is usually summarized as the doctrine of the Fatherhood of God. In its fuller statement it involves that account of the divine love for the individual man which is so characteristic and repeated a feature of the authentic sayings. The other thesis is what we now call judgment of value. It is the assertion of the infinite worth of each individual person, — an assertion richly illustrated in the parables, and used as the basis of the ethical teaching of Christ, since the value that God sets upon your brother is the deepest reason assigned to show why your own life should be one of love towards your brother.

VIII

So much for the barest suggestion of a teaching which you all know, and which I have not here further to expound. Our present question is simply this: Is this the whole of what is vital to Christianity? Or is there something vital which is not contained in these recorded sayings, so far as they relate to the matters just summarily mentioned?

The answer to this question is suggested by certain very well-known facts. First, these sayings are, in the master's mind, only part of a program which, as the event showed, related not only to the individual soul and its salvation, but to the reform of the whole existing and visible social order. Or, expressed in our modern terms, the teacher contemplated a social revolution, as well as the before-mentioned universal religious reformation of each individual life. He was led, at least towards the end of his career, to interpret his mission as that of the Messiah of his people. That the coming social revolution was conceived by him in divine and miraculous terms, that it was to be completed by the final judgment of all men, that the coming kingdom was to be not of this world, in the sense in which the Roman Empire was of this world, but was to rest upon the directly visible triumph of God's will through the miraculous appearance of the chosen messenger who should execute this will, — all this regarding the conception which was in Christ's mind seems clear. But, however the coming revolution was conceived, it was to be a violent and supernatural revolution of the external social order, and it was to appear openly to all men upon earth. The meek, the poor, were to inherit the earth; the mighty were to be cast down; the kingdoms of this world were to pass away; and the divine sovereignty was to take its visible place as the controller of all things.

Now it is no part of my present task to endeavor to state any theory as to why the master viewed his kingdom of heaven, in part at least, in this way. You may interpret the doctrine as the church has for ages done, as a doctrine relating to the far-off future end of all human affairs and to the supernatural mission of Christ as both Savior and Judge of the world; or you may view the revolutionary purposes of the master as I myself actually do, simply as his personal interpretation of the Messianic traditions of his people and of the social needs of his time and of the then common but mistaken expectation of the near end of the world. In any case, if this doctrine, however brought about or interpreted, was for the master a vital part of his teaching, then you have to view the resulting interpretation of life accordingly. I need not say, however, that whoever to-day can still find a place for the Messianic hopes and for the doctrine of the last judgment in his own interpretation of Christianity has once for all made up his mind to regard a doctrine, — and a deeply problematic doctrine, — a profoundly metaphysical doctrine about the person and work of Christ, and about the divine plan for the salvation of man, — as a vital part of his own Christianity.

And now, in this same connection, we can point out that, if the whole doctrine of Christ had indeed consisted for him in regarding the coming of the kingdom of heaven as identical with the inner transformation of each man by the spirit of divine love, then that direct and open opposition to the existing social authorities of his people which led to the Messianic tragedy would have been for the master simply needless. Christ chose this plan of open and social opposition for reasons of his own. We may interpret these reasons as the historical church has done, or we may view the matter otherwise, as I myself do. In any case, Christ's view of what was vital in Christianity certainly included, but also just as certainly went beyond, the mere preaching of the kingdom of heaven that is within you.

But one may still say, as many say who want to return to a purely primitive Christianity: Can *we* not choose to regard the religious doctrine of the parables and of the sayings, apart from the Messianic hopes and the anticipated social revolution, as for us vital and sufficient? Can we not decline to attempt to solve the Messianic mystery? Is it not for us enough to know simply that the master did indeed die for his faith, leaving his doctrine concerning the spiritual kingdom, concerning God the Father, and concerning man the beloved brother, as his final legacy to future generations? This legacy was of permanent value. Is it not enough for us?

I reply: To think thus is obviously to view Christ's doctrine as he himself did not view it. He certainly meant the kingdom of heaven to include the inner transformation of each soul by the divine love. But he also certainly conceived even this spiritual transformation in terms of some sort of Messianic mission, which was related to a miraculous coming transformation of human society. In the service of this Messianic social cause he died. And now even in Christ's interpretation of the inner and spiritual life of the individual man there are aspects which you cannot understand unless you view them in the light of the Messianic expectation. I refer to the master's doctrine upon that side of it which emphasizes the passive nonresistance of the individual man, in waiting for God's judgment. This side of Christ's doctrine has been frequently interpreted as requiring an extreme form of self-abnegation. It is this aspect of the doctrine which glorifies poverty as in itself an important aid to piety. In this sense, too, the master sometimes counsels a certain indifference to ordinary human social relations. In this same spirit his sayings so frequently illustrate the spirit of love by the mention of acts that involve the merely immediate relief of suffering, rather than by dwelling upon those more difficult and often more laborious forms of love, which his own life indeed exemplified, and which take the form of the lifelong service of a superpersonal social cause.

I would not for a moment wish to overemphasize the meaning of these negative and ascetic aspects of the sayings. Christ's ethical doctrine was unquestionably as much a positive individualism as it was a doctrine of love. It was also as genuinely a stern doctrine as it was a humane one. Nobody understands it who reduces it to mere self-abnegation, or to nonresistance, or to any form of merely sentimental amiability. Nevertheless, as it was taught, it included sayings and illustrations which have often been interpreted in the sense of pure asceticism, in the sense of simple nonresistance, in the sense of an unworldliness that seems opposed to the establishment and the prizing of definite humanities, — yes, even in the sense of an anarchical contempt for the forms of any present worldly social order. In brief, the doctrine contains a deep and paradoxical opposition between its central assertion of the infinite value of love and of every individual human soul, on the one hand, and those of its special teachings, on the other hand, which seem to express a negative attitude towards all our natural efforts to assert and to sustain the values of life by means of definite social coöperation, such as we men can by ourselves devise. Now the solution of this paradox seems plain when we remember the abnormal social conditions of those whom Christ was teaching, and interpret his message in the light of his Messianic social mission with its coming miraculous change of all human relations. But in that case an important part of the sayings must be viewed as possessing a meaning which is simply relative to the place, to the people, to the time, and to those Messianic hopes of an early end of the existing social order, — hopes which we know to have been mistakenly cherished by the early church.

I conclude, then, so far, that a simple return to a purely primitive Christianity as a body of doctrine complete in itself, directly and fully expressed in the sayings of Christ, and applicable, without notable supplement, to all times, and to our own day, — is an incomplete and therefore inadequate religious ideal. The spiritual kingdom of heaven, the transformation of the inner life which the sayings teach, is indeed a genuine part, — yes, a vital part, — of Christianity. But it is by no means the whole of what is vital to Christianity.

IX

I turn to the second of the answers to our main question. According to this answer, Christianity is a redemptive religion. What is most vital to Christianity is contained in whatever is essential and permanent about the doctrines of the incarnation and the atonement. Now this is the answer which, as you will by this time see, I myself regard as capable of an interpretation that will turn it into a correct answer to our question. In answering thus, I do not for a moment call in question the just-mentioned fact that the original teaching of the master regarding the kingdom of heaven is indeed a vital part of the whole of Christianity. But I do assert that this so-called purely primitive Christianity is not so vital, is not so central, is not so essential to mature Christianity as are the doctrines of the incarnation and the atonement when these are rightly interpreted. In the light of these doctrines alone can the work of the master be seen in its most genuine significance.

Yet, as has been already pointed out, the literal acceptance of this answer to our question, as many still interpret the answer, seems to be beset by serious difficulties. These difficulties are now easily summarized. The historical Christ of the sayings and the parables, little as we certainly know regarding his life, is still a definite and, in the main, an accessible object of study and of interpretation, just because, whatever else he was, he was the teacher of this recorded interpretation of life, — whether or not you regard that recorded interpretation as a fully complete and rounded whole. But the Christ whom the traditional doctrines of the atonement and of the incarnation present to us appears in the minds of most of us as the Christ of the legends of the early church, — a being whose nature and whose reported supernatural mission seem to be involved in doubtful mysteries — mysteries both theological and historical. Now I am not here to tell you in detail why the modern mind has come to be unwilling to accept, as literal reports of historical facts, certain well-known legends. I am not here to discuss that unwillingness upon its merits. It is enough for my present purpose to say first that the unwillingness exists, and, secondly, that, as a fact, I myself believe it to be a perfectly reasonable unwillingness. But I say this not at all because I suppose that modern insight has driven out of the reasonable world the reality of spiritual truth. The world of history is indeed a world full of the doubtful. And the whole world of phenomena in which you and I daily move about is a realm of mysteries. Nature and man, as we daily know them, and also daily misunderstand them, are not what they seem to us to be. The world of our usual human experience is but a beggarly fragment of the truth, and, if we take too seriously the bits of wisdom that it enables us to collect by the observation of special facts and of natural laws, it becomes a sort of curtain to hide from us the genuine realm of spiritual realities in the midst of which we all the while live. Moreover, it is one office of all higher religion to supplement these our fragments of experience and ordinary notions of the natural order by a truer, if still imperfect, interpretation of the spiritual realities that are beyond our present vision. That is, it is the business of religion to lift, however little, the curtain, to inspire us, not by mere dreams of ideal life, but by enlightening glimpses of the genuine truth which, if we were perfect, we should indeed see, not, as now, through a glass darkly, but face to face.

All this I hold to be true. And yet I fully share the modern unwillingness to accept legends as literally true. For it is not by first repeating the tale of mere marvels, of miracles, — by dwelling upon legends, and then by taking the accounts in question as literally true historical reports, — it is not thus that we at present, in our modern life, can best help ourselves to find our way to the higher world. These miraculous reports are best understood when we indeed first dwell upon them lovingly and meditatively, but thereupon learn to view them as symbols, as the products of the deep and endlessly instructive religious imagination, — and thereby learn to interpret the actually definite, and to my mind unquestionably superhuman and eternal, truth that these legends express, but express by figures, — in the form of a parable, an image, a narrative, a tale of some special happening. The tale is not literally true. But its deeper meaning may be absolutely true. In brief, I accept the opinion that it is the office of religion to interpret truths which are in themselves perfectly definite, eternal, and literal, but to interpret them to us by means of a symbolism which is the product of the constructive imagination of the great ages in which the religions which first voiced these truths grew up. There are some truths which our complicated natures best reach first through instinct and intuition, through parable and legend. Only when we have first reached them in this way, can most of us learn to introduce the practical and indeed saving application of these truths into our lives by living out the spirit of these parables. But then at last we may also hope, in the fullness of our own time, to comprehend these truths by a clearer insight into the nature of that eternal world which is indeed about and above us all, and which is the true source of our common life and light.

I am of course saying all this not as one having authority. I am simply indicating how students of philosophy who are of the type that I follow are accustomed to view these things. In this spirit I will now ask you to look for a moment at the doctrines of the incarnation and of the atonement in some of their deeper aspects. It is a gain thus to view the doctrines, whether or no you accept literally the well-known miraculous tale.

There has always existed in the Christian church a tradition tending to emphasize the conception that the supernatural work of Christ, which the church conceived in the form of the doctrines of the incarnation and the atonement, was not a work accomplished once for all at a certain historical point of time, but remains somehow an abiding work;

or, perhaps, that it ought to be viewed as a timeless fact, which never merely happened, but which is such as to determine anew in every age the relation of the faithful to God. Of course, the church has often condemned as heretical one or another form of these opinions. Nevertheless, such opinions have in fact entered into the formation of the official dogmas. An instance is the influence that such an interpretation had upon the historic doctrine of the Mass and of the real presence, — a doctrine which, as I have suggested, combines in one some of the most primitive of religious motives with some of the deepest religious ideas that men have ever possessed. In other less official forms, in forms which frequently approached, or crossed, the boundaries of technical heresy, some of the medieval mystics, fully believing in their own view of their faith, and innocent of any modern doubts about miracles, were accustomed in their tracts and sermons always and directly to interpret every part of the gospel narrative, including the miracles, as the expression of a vast and timeless whole of spiritual facts, whereof the narratives are merely symbols. In the sermons of Meister Eckhart, the great early German mystic, this way of preaching Christian doctrine is a regular part of his appeal to the people. I am myself in my philosophy no mystic, but I often wish that in our own days there were more who preached what is indeed vital in Christianity in somewhat the fashion of Eckhart. Let me venture upon one or two examples.

Eckhart begins as follows a sermon on the text, "Who is he that is born king of the Jews" (Matthew ii. 2): "Mark you," he says, "mark you concerning this birth, where it takes place. I say, as I have often said: This eternal birth takes place in the soul, and takes place there precisely as it takes place in the eternal world, — no more, no less. This birth happens in the essence, in the very foundation, of the soul." "All other creatures," he continues, "are God's footstool. But the soul is his image. This image must be adorned and fulfilled through this birth of God in the soul." The birth, the incarnation, of God occurs then, so Eckhart continues, in every soul, and eternally. But, as he hereupon asks: Is not this then also true of sinners, if this incarnation of God is thus everlasting and universal? Wherein lies then the difference between saint and sinner? What special advantage has the Christian from this doctrine of the incarnation? Eckhart instantly answers: Sin is simply due to the blindness of the soul to the eternal presence of the incarnate God. And that is what is meant by the passage: "The light shineth in the darkness, and the darkness comprehendeth it not."

Or again, Eckhart expounds in a sermon the statement that Christ came "in the fullness of time"; that is, as people usually and literally interpret the matter, Christ came when the human race was historically prepared for his coming. But Eckhart is careless concerning this historical and literal interpretation of the passage in question, although he doubtless also believes it. For him the true meaning of the passage is wholly spiritual. When, he asks in substance, is the day fulfilled? At the end of the day. When is a task fulfilled? When the task is over. When, therefore, is the fullness of time reached? Whenever a man is in his soul ready to be done with time; that is, when in contemplation he dwells only upon and in the eternal. Then alone, when the soul forgets time, and dwells upon God who is above time, then, and then only, does Christ really come. For Christ's coming means simply our becoming aware of what Eckhart calls the eternal birth; that is, the eternal relation of the real soul to the real God.

It is hard, in our times, to get any sort of hearing for such really deeper interpretations of what is indeed vital in Christianity. A charming, but essentially trivial, religious psychology to-day invites some of us to view religious experience simply as a chance play-at-hide-and-seek with certain so-called subliminal mental forces and processes, whose crudely capricious crises and catastrophes shall have expressed themselves in that feverish agitation that some take to be the essence of all. Meanwhile there are those who today try to keep religion alive mainly as a more or less medicinal influence, a sort of disinfectant or anodyne, that may perhaps still prove its value to a doubting world by curing dyspepsia, or by removing nervous worries. Over against such modern tendencies, — humane, but still, as interpretations of the true essence of religion, essentially trivial, — there are those who see no hope except in holding fast by a literal acceptance of tradition. There are, finally, those who undertake the task, lofty indeed, but still, as I think, hopeless, — the task of restoring what they call a purely primitive Christianity. Now I am no disciple of Eckhart; but I am sure that whatever is vital in Christianity concerns in fact the relation of the real individual human person to the real God. To the minds of the people whose religious tradition we have inherited this relation first came through the symbolic interpretation that the early church gave to the life of the master. It is this symbolic interpretation which is the historical legacy of the church. It is the genuine and eternal truth that lies behind this symbol which constitutes what is indeed vital to Christianity. I personally regard the supernatural narratives in which the church embodied its faith simply as symbols, — the product indeed of no man's effort to deceive, but of the religious imagination of the great constructive age of the early church. I also hold that the truth which lies behind these symbols is capable of a perfectly rational statement, that this statement lies in the direction which Eckhart, mistaken as he often was, has indicated to us. The truth in question is independent of the legends. It relates to eternal spiritual facts. I maintain also that those who, in various ages of the church, and in various ways, have tried to define and to insist upon what they have called the "Essential Christ," as distinguished from the historical Christ, have been nearing in various degrees the comprehension of what is vital in Christianity.

WHAT IS VITAL IN CHRISTIANITY?

X

What is true must be capable of expression apart from legends. What is eternally true may indeed come to our human knowledge through any event that happens to bring the truth in question to our notice; but, once learned, this truth may be seen to be independent of the historical events, whatever they were, which brought about our own insight. And the truth about the incarnation and the atonement seems to me to be statable in terms which I must next briefly indicate.

First, God, as our philosophy ought to conceive him, is indeed a spirit and a person; but he is not a being who exists in separation from the world, simply as its external creator. He expresses himself in the world; and the world is simply his own life, as he consciously lives it out. To use an inadequate figure, God expresses himself in the world as an artist expresses himself in the poems and the characters, in the music or in the other artistic creations, that arise within the artist's consciousness and that for him and in him consciously embody his will. Or again, God is this entire world, viewed, so to speak, from above and in its wholeness as an infinitely complex life which in an endless series of temporal processes embodies a single divine idea. You can indeed distinguish, and should distinguish, between the world as our common sense, properly but fragmentarily, has to view it, and as our sciences study it, — between this phenomenal world, I say, and God, who is infinitely more than any finite system of natural facts or of human lives can express. But this distinction between God and world means no separation. Our world is the fragmentary phenomenon that we see. God is the conscious meaning that expresses itself in and through the totality of all phenomena. The world, taken as a mass of happenings in time, of events, of natural processes, of single lives, is nowhere, and at no time, any complete expression of the divine will. But the entire world, of which our known world is a fragment, — the totality of what is, past, present, and future, the totality of what is physical and of what is mental, of what is temporal and of what is enduring, — this entire world is present at once to the eternal divine consciousness as a single whole, and this whole is what the absolute chooses as his own expression, and is what he is conscious of choosing as his own life. In this entire world God sees himself lived out. This world, when taken in its wholeness, is at once the object of the divine knowledge and the deed wherein is embodied the divine will. Like the Logos of the Fourth Gospel, this entire world is not only with God, but is God.

As you see, I state this doctrine, for the moment, quite summarily and dogmatically. Only an extensive and elaborate philosophical discussion could show you why I hold this doctrine to be true. Most of you, however, have heard of some such doctrine as the theory of the Divine Immanence. Some of you are aware that such an interpretation of the nature of God constitutes what is called philosophical Idealism. I am not here defending, nor even expounding, this doctrine. I believe, however, that this is the view of the divine nature which the church has always more or less intuitively felt to be true, and has tried to express, despite the fact that my own formulation of this doctrine includes some features which in the course of the past history of dogma have been upon occasion formally condemned as heresy by various church authorities. But for my part I had rather be a heretic, and appreciate the vital meaning of what the church has always tried to teach, than accept this or that traditional formulation, but be unable to grasp its religiously significant spirit.

Dogmatically, then, I state what, indeed, if there were time, I ought to expound and to defend on purely rational grounds. God and his world are one. And this unity is not a dead natural fact. It is the unity of a conscious life, in which, in the course of infinite time, a divine plan, an endlessly complex and yet perfectly definite spiritual idea, gets expressed in the lives of countless finite beings and yet with the unity of a single universal life.

Whoever hears this doctrine stated, asks, however, at once a question, — the deepest, and also the most tragic question of our present poor human existence: Why, then, if the world is the divine life embodied, is there so much evil in it, — so much darkness, ignorance, misery, disappointment, warfare, hatred, disease, death? — in brief, why is the world as we know it full of the unreasonable? Are all these gloomy facts but illusions, bad dreams of our finite existence, — facts unknown to the very God who is, and who knows, all truth? No, — that cannot be the answer; for then the question would recur: Why are these our endlessly tragic illusions permitted? Why are we allowed by the world-plan to be so unreasonable as to dream these bad dreams which fill our finite life, and which in a way constitute this finite life? And that question would then be precisely equivalent to the former question, and just as hard to solve. In brief, the problem of evil is the great problem that stands between our ordinary finite view and experience of life on the one hand and our consciousness of the reasonableness and the unity of the divine life on the other hand.

Has this problem of evil any solution? I believe that it has a solution, and that this solution has long since been in substance grasped and figured forth in symbolic forms by the higher religious consciousness of our race. This solution, not abstractly stated, but intuitively grasped, has also expressed itself in the lives of the wisest and best of the moral heroes of all races and nations of men. The value of suffering, the good that is at the heart of evil, lies in the spiritual triumphs that the endurance and the overcoming of evil can bring to those who learn the hard, the deep but glorious, lesson of life. And of all the spiritual triumphs that the presence of evil makes possible, the noblest is that which is won when a man is ready, not merely to bear the ills of fortune tranquilly if they come, as the Stoic moralists required their followers to do, but when one is willing to suffer vicariously, freely, devotedly, ills that he might have avoided, but that the cause to which he is loyal, and the errors and sins that he himself did not commit, call upon him to suffer in order that the world may be brought nearer to its destined union with the divine. In brief, as the mystics themselves often have said, sorrow — wisely encountered and freely borne — is one of the most precious privileges of the spiritual life. There is a certain lofty peace in triumphing over sorrow, which brings us to a consciousness of whatever is divine in life, in a way that mere joy, untroubled and unwon, can never make known to us. Perfect through suffering, — that is the universal, the absolutely necessary law of the higher spiritual life. It is a law that holds for God and for man, for those amongst men who have already become enlightened through learning the true lessons of their own sorrows, and for those who, full of hope, still look forward to a life from which they in the main anticipate joy and worldly success, and who have yet to learn that the highest good of life is to come to them through whatever willing endurance of hardness they, as good soldiers of their chosen loyal service, shall learn to choose or to endure as their offering to their sacred cause. This doctrine that I now state to you is indeed no ascetic doctrine. It does not for a moment imply that joy is a sin, or an evil symptom. What it does assert is that as long as the joys and successes which you seek are expected and sought by you simply as good fortune, which you try to win through mere cleverness — through mere technical skill in the arts of controlling fortune, — so long, I say, as this is your view of life, you know neither God's purpose nor the truth about man's destiny. Our always poor and defective skill in controlling fortune is indeed a valuable part of our reasonableness, since it is the natural basis upon which a higher spiritual life may be built. Hence the word, "Young men, be strong," and the common-sense injunction, "Be skillful, be practical," are good counsel. And so health, and physical prowess, and inner cheerfulness, are indeed wisely viewed as natural foundations for a higher life. But the higher life itself begins only when your health and your strength and your skill and your good cheer appear to you merely as talents, few or many, which you propose to devote, to surrender, to the divine order, to whatever ideal cause most inspires your loyalty, and gives sense and divine dignity to your life, — talents, I say, that you intend to return to your master with usury. And the work of the higher life consists, not in winning good fortune, but in transmuting all the transient values of fortune into eternal values. This you best do when you learn by experience how your worst fortune may be glorified, through wise resolve, and through the grace that comes from your conscious union with the divine, into something far better than any good fortune could give to you; namely, into a knowledge of how God himself endures evil, and triumphs over it, and lifts it out of itself, and wins it over to the service of good.

The true and highest values of the spiritual

world consist, I say, in the triumph over suffering, over sorrow, and over unreasonableness; and the triumph over these things may appear in our human lives in three forms: First, as mere personal fortitude, — as the stoical virtues in their simplest expression. The stoical virtues are the most elementary stage of the higher spiritual life. Fortitude is indeed required of every conscious agent who has control over himself at all. And fortitude, even in this simplest form as manly and strenuous endurance, teaches you eternal values that you can never learn unless you first meet with positive ills of fortune, and then force yourself to bear them in the loyal service of your cause. Willing endurance of suffering and grief is the price that you have to pay for conscious fidelity to any cause that is vast enough to be worthy of the loyalty of a lifetime. And thus no moral agent can be made perfect except through suffering borne in the service of his cause. Secondly, the triumph over suffering appears in the higher form of that conscious union with the divine plan which occurs when you learn that love, and loyalty, and the idealizing of life, and the most precious and sacred of all human relationships, are raised to their highest levels, are glorified, only when we not merely learn in our own personal case to suffer, to sorrow, to endure, and be spiritually strong, but when we learn to do these things together with our own brethren. For the comradeship of those who willingly practice fortitude not merely as a private virtue, but as brethren in sorrow, is a deeper, a sweeter, a more blessed comradeship than ever is that of the lovers who have not yet been tried so as by fire. Then the deepest trials of life come to you and your friend together; and when, after the poor human heart has indeed endured what for the time it is able to bear of anguish, it finds its little moment of rest, and when you are able once more to clasp the dear hand that would help if it could, and to look afresh into your friend's eyes and to see there the light of love as you could never see it before, — then, even in the darkness of this world, you catch some faint far-off glimpse of how the spirit may yet triumph despite all, and of why sorrow may reveal to us, as we sorrow and endure together, what we should never have known of life, and of love, and of each other, and of the high places of the spirit, if this cup had been permitted to pass from us. But thirdly, and best, the triumph of the spirit over suffering is revealed to us not merely when we endure, when we learn through sorrow to prize our brethren more, and when we learn to see new powers in them and even in our poor selves, powers such as only sorrow could bring to light, — but when we also turn back from such experiences to real life again, remembering that sorrow's greatest lesson is the duty of offering ourselves more than ever to the practical service of some divine cause in this world. When one is stung to the heart and seemingly wholly overcome by the wounds of fortune, it sometimes chances that he learns after a while to arise from his agony, with the word: "Well then, if, whether by my own fault or without it, I must descend into hell,

I will remember that in this place of sorrow there are the other souls in torment, seeking light; I will help them to awake and arise. As I enter I will open the gates of hell that they may go forth." Whatever happens to me, I say, this is a possible result of sorrow. I have known those men and women who could learn such a lesson from sorrow and who could practice it. These are the ones who, coming up through great tribulation, show us the highest glimpse that we have in this life of the triumph of the spirit over sorrow. But these are the ones who are willing to suffer vicariously, to give their lives as a ransom for many. These tell us what atonement means.

Well, these are, after all, but glimpses of truth. But they show us why the same law holds for all the highest spiritual life. They show us that God too must sorrow in order that he may triumph.

Now the true doctrine of the incarnation and of the atonement is, in its essence, simply the conception of God's nature which this solution of the problem of evil requires. First,

God expresses himself in this world of finitude, incarnates himself in this realm of human imperfection, but does so in order that through finitude and imperfection, and sorrow and temporal loss, he may win in the eternal world (that is, precisely, in the conscious unity of his whole life) his spiritual triumph over evil. In this triumph consists his highest good, and ours. It is God's true and eternal triumph that speaks to us through the well-known word: "In this world ye shall have tribulation. But fear not; I have overcome the world." Mark, I do not say that we, just as we naturally are, are already the true and complete incarnation of God. No, it is in overcoming evil, in rising above our natural unreasonableness, in looking towards the divine unity, that we seek what Eckhart so well expressed when he said, Let God be born in the soul. Hence the doctrine of the incarnation is no doctrine of the natural divinity of man. It is the doctrine which teaches that the world will desires our unity with the universal purpose, that God will be born in us and through our consent, that the whole meaning of our life is that it shall transmute transient and temporal values into eternal meanings. Humanity becomes conscious God incarnate only in so far as humanity looks godwards; that is, in the direction of the whole unity of the rational spiritual life.

And now, secondly, the true doctrine of the atonement seems to me simply this: We, as we temporally and transiently are, are destined to win our union with the divine only through learning to triumph over our own evil, over the griefs of fortune, over the unreasonableness and the sin that now beset us. This conquest we never accomplish alone. As the mother that bore you suffered, so the world suffers for you and through and in you until you win your peace in union with the divine will. Upon such suffering you actually depend for your natural existence, for the toleration which your imperfect self constantly demands from the world, for the help that your helplessness so often needs. When you sorrow, then, remember that God sorrows, — sorrows in you, since in all your finitude you still are part of his life; sorrows for you, since it is the intent of the divine spirit, in the plan of its reasonable world, that you should not remain what you now are; and sorrows, too, in waiting for higher fulfillment, since indeed the whole universe needs your spiritual triumph for the sake of its completion.

On the other hand, this doctrine of the atonement means that there is never any completed spiritual triumph over sorrow which is not accompanied with the willingness to suffer vicariously; that is, with the will not merely to endure bravely, but to force one's very sorrow to be an aid to the common cause of all mankind, to give one's life as a ransom for one's cause, to use one's bitterest and most crushing grief as a means towards the raising of all life to the divine level. It is not enough to endure. Your duty is to make your grief a source of blessing. Thus only can sorrow bring you into conscious touch with the universal life.

Now all this teaching is old. The church

began to learn its own version of this solution of the problem of evil when first it sorrowed over its lost master; when first it began to say: "It was needful that Christ should suffer"; when first in vision and in legend it began to conceive its glorified Lord. When later it said, "In the God-man Christ God suffered, once for all and in the flesh, to save us; in him alone the Word became flesh and dwelt among us," the forms of its religious imagination were transient, but the truth of which these forms were the symbol was everlasting. And we sum up this truth in two theses: First, God wins perfection through expressing himself in a finite life and triumphing over and through its very finitude. And secondly, Our sorrow is God's sorrow. God means to express himself by winning us through the very triumph over evil to unity with the perfect life; and therefore our fulfillment, like our existence, is due to the sorrow and the triumph of God himself. These two theses express, I believe, what is vital in Christianity.

ESSAY IV

THE PROBLEM OF TRUTH IN THE LIGHT OF RECENT DISCUSSION

ESSAY IV

THE PROBLEM OF TRUTH IN THE LIGHT OF RECENT DISCUSSION [1]

THE question: What is Truth? is a typical philosophical problem. But it has been by no means at all times equally prominent throughout the history of philosophy. The ages in which it has come to the front have been those wherein, as at present, a keenly critical spirit has been predominant. At such times metaphysical interests are more or less subordinated, for a while, to the problems about method, to logical researches, or to the investigations which constitute a Theory of Knowledge.

Such periods, as we know, have recurred more than once since scholastic philosophy declined. And such a period was that which Kant dominated. But the sort of inquiry

[1] An address delivered before the International Congress of Philosophy at Heidelberg, in September, 1908.

into the nature of truth which Kant's doctrine initiated quickly led, at the close of the eighteenth century, to a renewed passion for metaphysical construction. The problem regarding the nature of truth still occupied a very notable place in the doctrine of Fichte. It constituted one of the principal concerns, also, of Hegel's so much neglected and ill-understood "Phänomenologie des Geistes." And yet both in the minds of the contemporaries of Fichte and of Hegel, and still more in those of their later disciples and opponents, the problem of truth went again into the background when compared with the metaphysical, the ethical, and the theological interests which constructive idealism and its opponents, in those days, came to represent. Hence wherever one looks, in the history of philosophical opinion between 1830 and 1870, one sees how the problem of truth, although never wholly neglected, still remained, for some decades, out of the focus of philosophical interest.

But the scene rapidly changed about and after the year 1870. Both the new psychology and the new logic, which then began to flourish, seemed, erelong, almost equally to emphasize the importance of a reconsideration of the problem as to the nature of truth. These doctrines did this, especially because the question whether logic was henceforth to be viewed as a part of psychology became once more prominent, so soon as the psychological researches then undertaken had attracted the strong interest of the philosophical public. And meanwhile the revived interest in Kant, growing, as it did, side by side with the new psychology, called for a reinterpretation of the problems of the critical philosophy. The reawakening of Idealism, in England and in America, called attention, in its own way, to the same problem. The modern philosophical movement in France, — a movement which was, from the outset, almost equally made up of a devotion to the new psychology and of an interest in the philosophy of the sciences, has coöperated in insisting upon the need of a revision of the theory of truth. And to complete the story of the latest philosophy, recent tendencies in ethics, emphasizing as they have done the problems of individualism, and demanding a far-reaching reconsideration of the whole nature of moral truth, have added the weight of their own, often passionate, interest to the requirements which are here in question.

The total result is that we are just now in the storm and stress of a reëxamination of the whole problem of truth. About this problem the philosophical interest of to-day centers. Consequently, whether you discuss the philosophy of Nietzsche or of mathematics, — whether the *Umwertung aller Werte* or the "class of all classes," — whether Mr. Russell's "Contradiction" or the *Uebermensch* is in question, — or whether none of these things attract you at all, so that your inquiries relate to psychology, or to evolution, or to the concepts of the historical sciences, or to whatever other region of philosophy you please, — always the same general issue has sooner or later to be faced. You are involved in some phase of the problem about the nature of truth.

So much, then, as a bare indication of the historical process which has led us into our present position. I propose, in the present address, to offer an interpretation of some of the lessons that, as I think, we may learn from the recent discussions of the problem whose place in all our minds I have thus indicated.

I

It seems natural to begin such a discussion by a classification of the main motives which are represented by the principal recent theories regarding the nature of truth. In enumerating these motives I need not dwell, in this company, upon those historical inferences and traditions whose presence in recent thought is most easily and universally recognized. That Empiricism, — due to the whole history of the English school, modified in its later expressions by the Positivism of a former generation, and by the types of Naturalism which have resulted from the recent progress of the special sciences, — that, I say, such empiricism has affected our modern discussion of the nature of truth, — this we all recognize. I need not insist upon this fact. Moreover, the place which Kant occupies in the history of the theory of truth, — that again is something which it is needless here to emphasize. And that the teaching of Fichte and of Hegel, as well as still other idealistic traditions, are also variously represented by present phases of opinion regarding our problem, we shall not now have to rehearse. I presuppose, then, these historical commonplaces. It is not, however, in terms of these that I shall now try to classify the motives to which the latest theories of truth are due.

These recent motives, viewed apart from those unquestionably real influences of the older traditions of the history of philosophy are, to my mind, three in number:

First, there is the motive especially suggested to us modern men by the study of the history of institutions, by our whole interest in what are called evolutionary processes, and by a large part of our recent psychological investigation. This is the motive which leads many of us to describe human life altogether as a more or less progressive adjustment to a natural environment. This motive incites us, therefore, to judge all human products and all human activities as instruments for the preservation and enrichment of man's natural existence. Of late this motive, whose modern forms are extremely familiar, has directly affected the theory of truth. The result appears in a part, although not in the whole, of what the doctrines known as Instrumentalism, Humanism, and Pragmatism have been of late so vigorously teaching, in England, in America, in Italy, in France, and, in still other forms, in Germany.

From the point of view which this motive suggests, human opinions, judgments, ideas, are part of the effort of a live creature to adapt himself to his natural world. Ideas and beliefs are, in a word, organic functions. And truth, in so far as we men can recognize truth at all, is a certain value belonging to such ideas. But this value itself is simply like the value which any natural organic function possesses. Ideas and opinions are instruments whose use lies in the fact that, if they are the right ones, they preserve life and render life stable. Their existence is due to the same natural causes that are represented in our whole organic evolution. Accordingly, assertions or ideas are true in proportion as they accomplish this their biological and psychological function. The value of truth is itself a biological and psychological value. The true ideas are the ones which adapt us for life as human beings. Truth, therefore, grows with our growth, changes with our needs, and is to be estimated in accordance with our success. The result is that all truth is as relative as it is instrumental, as human as it is useful.

The motive which recent Instrumentalism or Pragmatism expresses, in so far as it takes this view of the nature of truth, is of course in one sense an ancient motive. Every cultivated nation, upon beginning to think, recognizes in some measure such a motive. The Greeks knew this motive, and deliberately connected both the pursuit and the estimate of truth with the art of life in ways whose problematic aspects the Sophists already illustrated. Socrates and his followers, and later the Stoics as well as the Epicureans, also considered, in their various ways, this instrumental aspect of the nature of truth. And even in the Hindoo Upanishads one can find instances of such humanistic motives influencing the inquiry into the problem of truth. But it is true that the historical science of the nineteenth century, beginning, as it did, with its elaborate study of the history of institutions, and culminating in the general doctrines regarding evolution, has given to this motive an importance and a conscious definiteness such as makes its recent embodiment in Pragmatism a very modern and, in many ways, a novel doctrine about the nature of truth.

II

But closely bound up with this first motive in our recent thinking there is a second motive, which in several ways very strongly contrasts with the first. Yet in many minds these two motives are so interwoven that the writers in question are unaware which motive they are following when they utter their views about the nature of truth. No doubt one may indeed recognize the contrast between these motives, and may, nevertheless, urge good reasons for following in some measure both of them, each in its own way. Yet whoever blindly confuses them is inevitably led into hopeless contradictions. As a fact, a large number of our recent pragmatists have never learned consciously to distinguish them. Yet they are indeed easy to distinguish, however hard it may be to see how to bring them into a just synthesis.

This second motive is the same as that which, in ethics, is responsible for so many sorts of recent Individualism. It is the motive which in the practical realm Nietzsche glorified. It is the longing to be self-possessed and inwardly free, the determination to submit to no merely external authority. I need not pause to dwell upon the fact that, in its application to the theory of truth, precisely as in its well-known applications to ethics, this motive is Protean. Every one of us is, I suppose, more or less under its influence.

Sometimes, this motive appears mainly as a skeptical motive. Then it criticizes, destructively, traditional truth and thereupon leaves us empty of all assurances. But sometimes it assumes the shape of a sovereign sort of rationalism, whereby the thinking subject, first rebelling against outer authority, creates his own laws, but then insists that all others shall obey these laws. In other cases, however, it takes the form of a purely subjective idealism, confident of its own but claiming no authority. Or again, with still different results, it consciously unites its ethical with its theoretical interests, calls itself "Personal Idealism," and regards as its main purpose, not only the freeing of the individual from all spiritual bondage, theoretical and practical, but also the winning for him of an inner harmony of life. In general, in its highest as in some of its less successful embodiments, when it considers the sort of truth that we ought most to pursue, this motive dwells, as Professor Eucken has so effectively taught it to dwell, upon the importance of a *Lebensanschauung* as against the rigidity and the pretended finality of a mere *Weltanschauung*.

But meanwhile, upon occasion, this same motive embodies itself in various tendencies of the sort known as Irrationalism. In this last case, it points out to us how the intelligence, after all, is but a single and a very narrow function of our nature, which must not be allowed to supersede or even too much to dominate the rest of our complex and essentially obscure, if fascinating, life. Perhaps, on the very highest levels of life, as it hereupon suggests to us: *Gefühl ist alles*. If not, then at all events, we have the alternative formula: *Im Anfang war die Tat*. Or, once again, the solving word of the theory of truth is Voluntarism. Truth is won by willing, by creative activities. The doer, or perhaps the deed, not only finds, but *is*, the truth. Truth is not to be copied, but to be created. It is living truth. And life is action.

I have thus attempted to indicate, by well-known phrases, the nature of this second motive, — one whose presence in our recent theories of truth I believe that you will all recognize. Despite the Protean character and (as you will all at once see) the mutually conflicting characters of its expressions, you will observe, I think, its deeper unity, and also its importance as an influence in our age. With us at present it acts as a sort of ferment, and also as an endless source of new enterprises. It awakens us to resist the most various kinds of doctrinal authority, — scientific, clerical, academic, popular. It inspires countless forms of Modernism, both within and without the boundaries of the various confessions of Christendom. As an effective motive, one finds it upon the lowest as also upon the highest levels of our intellectual and moral life. In some sense, as I have said, we all share it. It is the most characteristic and the most problematic of the motives of the modern world. Anarchism often appeals to it; yet the most saintly form of devotion, the most serious efforts for the good of mankind, and our sternest and loftiest spiritual leaders, agree in employing it, and in regarding it as in some sense sacred.

Our age shares this motive with the age of the French Revolution, of the older Idealistic movement, and of the Romantic School. All the more unfortunate, as I think, is the fact that many who glory in the originality of their own recent opinions about the nature of truth, know so little of the earlier history of this motive, read so seldom the lesson of the past, and are thus so ill-prepared to appreciate both the spiritual dignity and the pathetic paradox of this tendency to make the whole problem of truth identical with the problem of the rights and the freedom of the individual.

III

I turn herewith to the third of the motives that I have to enumerate. In its most general form it is a very ancient and familiar motive.

It is, indeed, very different from both of the foregoing. Superficially regarded, it seems, at first sight, less an expression of interests that appear ethical. At heart, however, it is quite as deep a motive as either of the others, and it is in fact a profoundly ethical motive as well as a genuinely intellectual one. One may say that, in a sense and to some degree, it pervades the whole modern scientific movement, is present wherever two or three are gathered together for a serious exchange of scientific opinions, and is, in most cases, the one motive that, in scientific assemblies, is more or less consciously in mind whenever somebody present chances to refer to the love of truth, or to the scientific conscience of his hearers.

I have called this third on our list of motives an ancient motive. It is so. Yet in modern times it has assumed very novel forms, and has led to scientific and, in the end, to philosophical enterprises which, until recently, nobody would have thought possible.

It would be unwise at this point to attempt

to define this motive in abstract terms. I must first exemplify it. When I say that it is the motive to which the very existence of the exact sciences is due, and when I add the remark that our scientific common sense knows this motive as the fondness for dispassionately weighing evidence, and often simply names it the love of objectivity, I raise more questions in your minds regarding the nature of this motive than at this point I can answer. If, however, anybody suggests, say from the side of some form of recent pragmatism, that I must be referring to the nowadays so deeply discredited motives of a pure "Intellectualism," I repudiate at once the suggestion. The motive to which I refer is intensely practical. Men have lived and died for it, and have found it inestimably precious. I know of no motive purer or sweeter in human life. Meanwhile, it indeed chances to be the motive which has partially embodied itself in Pure Mathematics. And neither the tribe of Nietzsche nor the kindred of the instrumentalists have been able justly to define it.

IN THE LIGHT OF DISCUSSION

What I am just now interested to point out is that this motive has entered, in very novel ways, into the formulation of certain modern theories of truth. And when I speak of its most novel forms of expression, the historical process to which I refer is the development of the modern critical study of the foundations of mathematics.

To philosophical students in general the existence of metageometrical researches, which began at the outset of the nineteenth century, has now been made fairly familiar. But the non-Euclidean geometry is but a small fragment of that investigation of the foundations of mathematical truth which went on so rapidly during the nineteenth century. Among the most important of the achievements of the century in this direction were the new definitions of continuity and the irrational numbers, the modern exact theory of limits, and the still infant theory of Assemblages. Most important of all, to my mind, were certain discoveries in the field of Logic of which I shall later say a word. I mention these matters here as examples of the influence of a motive whose highly technical applications may make it seem to one at a distance hopelessly intellectualistic, but whose relation to the theory of truth is close, just because, as I think, its relation to truly ethical motives is also extremely intimate.

The motive in question showed itself at the outset of the nineteenth century, and later in the form of an increased conscientiousness regarding what should be henceforth accepted as a rigid proof in the exact sciences. The Greek geometers long ago invented the conception of rigid methods of proof and brought their own methods, in certain cases, very near to perfection. But the methods that they used proved to be inapplicable to many of the problems of modern mathematics. The result was that, in the seventeenth and eighteenth centuries, the mathematical sciences rapidly took possession of new realms of truth, but in doing so sacrificed much of the old classic rigidity. Nevertheless, regarded as the instrumentalists now desire us to regard truth, the mathematical methods of the eighteenth century were indeed incomparably more successful in adjusting the work of the physical sciences to the demands of experience than the methods of the Greek geometers had ever been. If instrumentalism had been the whole story of man's interest in truth, the later developments would have been impossible. Nevertheless the modern scientific conscience somehow became increasingly dissatisfied with its new mathematical possessions. It regarded them as imperfectly won. It undertook to question, in a thousand ways, its own methods and its own presuppositions. It learned to reject altogether methods of proof which, for a time, had satisfied the greatest constructive geniuses of earlier modern mathematics. The result has been the development of profoundly novel methods, both of research and of instruction in the exact sciences. These methods have in many ways brought to a still higher perfection the Greek ideal of rigid proof. Yet the same methods have shown themselves to be no mere expressions of a pedantic intellectualism. They have meant clearness, self-possession, and a raising of the scientific conscience to higher levels. Meanwhile, they proved potent both in conquering new realms and in discovering the wonderful connections that we now find linking together types of exact truth which at first sight appeared to be hopelessly diverse.

In close union with the development of these new methods in the exact sciences, and, as I may say, in equally close union with this new scientific conscience, there has gradually come into being a reformed Logic, — a logic still very imperfectly expounded in even the best modern textbooks, and as yet hardly grasped, in its unity, by any one investigator, — but a logic which is rapidly progressing, which is full of beauty, and which is destined, I believe, profoundly to influence, in the near future, our whole philosophy of truth. This new logic appears to offer to us an endless realm for detailed researches. As a set of investigations it is as progressive as any instrumentalist can desire. The best names for it, I think, are the names employed by several different thinkers who have contributed to its growth. Our American logician, Mr. Charles Peirce, named it, years ago, the Logic of Relatives. Mr. Russell has called it the Logic, or the Calculus, of Relations. Mr. Kempe has proposed to entitle it the Theory of Mathematical Form. One might also call it a new and general theory of the Categories. Seen from a distance, as I just said, it appears to be a collection of highly technical special researches, interesting only to a few. But when one comes into closer contact with any one of its serious researches, one sees that its main motive is such as to interest every truthful and reflective inquirer who really grasps that motive, while the conception of truth which it forces upon our attention is a conception which neither of the other motives just characterized can be said adequately to express.

In so far as the new logic has up to this time given shape to philosophical theories of truth, it in part appears to tend towards what the pragmatists nowadays denounce as Intellectualism. As a fact Mr. Bertrand Russell, the brilliant and productive leader of this movement in England, and his philosophical friend Mr. George Moore, seem to regard their own researches as founded upon a sort of new Realism, which views truth as a realm wholly independent of the constructive activities by which we ourselves find or pursue truth. But the fact that Mr. Charles Peirce, one of the most inventive of the creators of the new logic, is also viewed by the Pragmatists as the founder of their own method, shows how the relation of the new logic to the theory of truth is something that still needs to be made clear. As a fact, I believe that the outcome of the new logic will be a new synthesis of Voluntarism and Absolutism.

What I just now emphasize is, that this modern revision of the concepts of the exact sciences, and this creation of a new logic, are in any case due to a motive which is at once theoretical and ethical. It is a motive which has defined standards of rigidity in proof such as were, until recently, unknown. In this sense it has meant a deepening and quickening of the scientific conscience. It has also seemed, in so far, to involve a rejection of that love of expediency in thinking which is now a favorite watchword of pragmatists and instrumentalists. And when viewed from this side the new logic obviously tends to emphasize some form of absolutism, to reject relativism in thinking, to make sterner requirements upon our love of truth than can be expressed in terms of instrumentalism or of individualism. And yet the motive which lies beneath this whole movement has been, I insist, no barren intellectualism. The novelty of the constructions to which this motive has led, — the break with tradition which the new geometry (for instance) has involved, — such things have even attracted, from a distance, the attention of some of the least exactly trained of the pragmatist thinkers, and have aroused their hasty and uncomprehending sympathy. "This non-Euclidean geometry," they have said, "these novel postulates, these '*freie Schöpfungen des menschlichen Geistes*' (as Dedekind, himself one of the great creative minds of the new logical movement, has called the numbers), — well, surely these must be instances in favor of *our* theory of truth. Thus, as we should have predicted, novelties appear in what was supposed to be an absolutely fixed region. Thus (as Professor James words the matter), human thought 'boils over,' and ancient truths alter, grow, or decay." Yet when modern pragmatists and relationists use such expressions, they fail to comprehend the fact that the new discoveries in these logical and mathematical fields simply exemplify a *more* rigid concept of truth than ever, before the new movement began, had been defined in the minds of the mathematicians themselves. The non-Euclidean geometry, strange to say, is not a discovery that we are any freer than we were before to think as we like regarding the system of geometrical truth. It is one part only of what Hilbert has called the "logical analysis" of our concept of space. When we take this analysis as a whole, it involves a deeper insight than Euclid could possibly possess into the unchangeable necessities which bind together the system of logical relationships that the space of our experience merely exemplifies. Nothing could be more fixed than are these necessities. As for the numbers, which Dedekind called "*freie Schöpfungen*," — well, his own masterpiece of logical theory is a discovery and a rigid demonstration of a very remarkable and thoroughly objective truth about the fundamental relations in terms of which we all of us do our thinking. His proof that all of the endless wealth of the properties of the ordinal numbers follows from a certain synthesis of two of the simplest of our logical conceptions, neither one of which, when taken alone, seems to have anything to do with the conception of order or of number, — this proof, I say, is a direct contribution to a systematic theory of the categories, and, as such, is, to the logical inquirer, a dramatically surprising discovery of a realm of objective truth, which nobody is free to construct or to abandon at his pleasure. If this be relativism, it is the relativism of an eternal system of relations. If this be freedom, it is the divine freedom of a self-determined, but, for that very reason, absolutely necessary fashion of thought and of activity.

Well, — to sum up, — this third motive in modern inquiry has already led us to the discovery of what are, for us, novel truths regarding the fundamental relations upon which all of our thought and all of our activity rest. These newly discovered truths possess an absoluteness which simply sets at naught the empty trivialities of current relativism. Such truth has, in fact, the same sort of relation to the biologically "instrumental" value of our thinking processes as the Theory of Numbers (that "divine science," as Gauss called it) has to the account books of the shopkeeper.

And yet, as I must insist, the motive that has led us to this type of absolutism is no pure intellectualism. And the truth in question is as much a truth about our modes of activity as the purest voluntarism could desire it to be. In brief, there is, I believe, an absolute voluntarism, a theory of the way in which activities must go on if they go on at all. And, as I believe, just such a theory is that which in future is to solve for us the problem of the nature of truth.

I have illustrated our third motive at length. Shall I now try to name it? Well, I should say that it is at bottom the same motive that lay at the basis of Kant's Critical Philosophy; but it is this motive altered by the influence of the modern spirit. It is the motive which leads us to seek for clear and exact self-consciousness regarding the principles both of our belief and of our conduct. This motive leads us to be content only in case we can indeed find principles of knowledge and of action, — principles, not mere transient expediences, and not mere caprices. On the other hand, this motive bids us decline to accept mere authority regarding our principles. It requires of us freedom along with insight, exactness side by side with assurance, and self-criticism as well as search for the ultimate.

IV

In thus sketching for you these three motives, I have been obliged to suggest my estimate of their significance. But this estimate has so far been wholly fragmentary. Let me next indicate the sense in which I believe that each of these three motives tends, in a very important sense, to throw light upon the genuine theory of truth.

I begin here with the first of the three motives, — namely, with the motive embodied in recent instrumentalism. Instrumentalism views truth as simply the value belonging to certain ideas in so far as these ideas are biological functions of our organisms, and psychological functions whereby we direct our choices and attain our successes.

Wide and manifold are the inductive evidences which the partisans of such theories of truth adduce in support of their theory. There is the evidence of introspection and of the modern psychological theory of the understanding. Opinions, beliefs, ideas, — what are they all but accompaniments of the motor processes whereby, as a fact, our organisms are adjusted to their environment? To discover the truth of an idea, what is that for any one of us but to observe our success in our adjustment to our situation? Knowledge is power. Common sense long ago noted this fact. Empiricism has also since taught us that we deal only with objects of experience. The new instrumentalism adds to the old empiricism simply the remark that we possess truth in so far as we learn how to control these objects of experience. And to this more direct evidence for the instrumental theory of truth is added the evidence derived from the whole work of the modern sciences. In what sense are scientific hypotheses and theories found to be true? Only in this sense, says the instrumentalist, — only in this sense, that through these hypotheses we acquire constantly new sorts of control over the course of our experience. If we turn from scientific to moral truth, we find a similar result. The moral ideas of any social order are practical plans and practical demands in terms of which this social order endeavors, by controlling the activities of its members, to win general peace and prosperity. The truth of moral ideas lies solely in this their empirical value in adjusting individual activities to social demands, and in thus winning general success for all concerned.

Such are mere hints of the evidences that can be massed to illustrate the view that the truth of ideas is actually tested, and is to be tested, by their experienced workings, by their usefulness in enabling man to control his empirically given situation. If this be the case, then truth is always relative to the men concerned, to their experience, and to their situations. Truth grows, changes, and refuses to be tested by absolute standards. It *happens* to ideas, in so far as they *work*. It belongs to them when one views them as instruments to an end. The result of all this is a relativistic, an evolutionary, theory of truth. For such a view logic is a part of psychology, — a series of comments upon certain common characteristics of usefully working ideas and opinions. Ethical theory is a branch of evolutionary sociology. And in general, if you want to test the truth of ideas and opinions, you must look forward to their workings, not backward to the principles from which they might be supposed to follow, nor yet upwards to any absolute standards which may be supposed to guide them, and least of all to any realm of fixed facts that they are supposed to be required, willy nilly, to copy. Truth is no barren repetition of a dead reality, but belongs, as a quality, to the successful deeds by which we produce for ourselves the empirical realities that we want.

Such is the sort of evidence which my friends, Professor James and Professor Dewey, and their numerous followers, in recent discussion, have advanced in favor of this instrumental, practical, and evolutionary theory of truth. Such are the considerations which, in other forms, Mach has illustrated by means of his history and analyses of the work of modern science.

THE PROBLEM OF TRUTH

Our present comment upon this theory must be given in a word. It contains indeed a report of the truth about our actual human life, and about the sense in which we all seek and test and strive for truth, precisely in so far as truth-seeking is indeed a part of our present organic activities. But the sense in which this theory is thus indeed a true account of a vast range of the phenomena of human life is not reducible to the sense which the theory itself ascribes to the term "truth."

For suppose I say, reporting the facts of the history of science: "Newton's theory of gravitation proved to be true, and its truth lay in this: The definition and the original testing of the theory consisted in a series of the organic and psychological functions of the live creature Newton. His theories were for him true in so far as, after hard work, to be sure, and long waiting, they enabled him to control and to predict certain of his own experiences of the facts of nature. The same theories are still true for us because they have successfully guided, and still guide, certain observations and experiences of the men of to-day." This statement reduces the truth of Newton's theory to the type of truth which instrumentalism demands. But in what sense is my account of this matter itself a true account of the facts of human life? Newton is dead. As mortal man he succeeds no longer. His ideas, as psychological functions, died with him. His earthly experiences ceased when death shut his eyes. Wherein consists to-day, then, the historical truth that Newton ever existed at all, or that the countless other men whom his theories are said to have guided ever lived, or experienced, or succeeded? And if I speak of the men of to-day, in what sense is the statement true that they now live, or have experience, or use Newton's theory, or succeed with it as an instrument? No doubt all these historical and socially significant statements of mine are indeed substantially true. But does their truth consist in my success in using the ideal instruments that I use when I utter these assertions? Evidently I mean, by calling these my own assertions true, much more than I can interpret in terms of my experience of their success in guiding my act.

In brief, the truth that historical events ever happened at all; the truth that there ever was a past time, or that there ever will be a future time; the truth that anybody ever succeeds, except in so far as I myself, just now, in the use of these my present instruments for the transient control of my passing experience chance to succeed; the truth that there is any extended course of human experience at all, or any permanence, or any long-lasting success, — well, all such truths, they are indeed true, but their truth cannot possibly consist in the instrumental value which any man ever experiences as belonging to any of his own personal ideas or acts. Nor can this truth consist in anything that even a thousand or a million men can separately experience, each as the success of his own ideal instruments. For no one man experiences the success of any man but himself, or of any instruments but his own; and the truth, say, of Newton's theory consists, by hypothesis, in the perfectly objective fact that generations of men have really succeeded in guiding their experience by this theory. But that this is the fact no man, as an individual man, ever has experienced or will experience under human conditions.

When an instrumentalist, then, gives to us his account of the empirical truth that men obtain through using their ideas as instruments to guide and to control their own experience, his account of human organic and psychological functions may be, — yes, is, — as far as it goes, true. But if it is true at all, then it is true as an account of the characters actually common to the experience of a vast number of men. It is true, if at all, as a report of the objective constitution of a certain totality of facts which we call human experience. It is, then, true in a sense which no man can ever test by the empirical success of his own ideas as his means of controlling his own experiences. Therefore the truth which we must ascribe to instrumentalism, if we regard it as a true doctrine at all, is precisely a truth, not in so far as instrumentalism is itself an instrument for helping on this man's or that man's way of controlling his experience. If instrumentalism is true, it is true as a report of facts about the general course of history, of evolution, and of human experience, — facts which transcend every individual man's experience, verifications, and successes. To make its truth consist in the mere sum of the various individual successes is equally vain, unless indeed that sum is a fact. But no individual man ever experiences that fact.

Instrumentalism, consequently, expresses no motive which by itself alone is adequate to constitute any theory of truth. And yet, as I have pointed out, I doubt not that instrumentalism gives such a substantially true account of man's natural functions as a truth seeker. Only the sense in which instrumentalism is a true account of human life is opposed to the adequacy of its own definition of truth. The first of our three motives is, therefore, useful only if we can bring it into synthesis with other motives. In fact it is useless to talk of the success of the human spirit in its efforts to win control over experience, unless there is indeed a human spirit which is more than any man's transient consciousness of his own efforts, and unless there is an unity of experience, an unity objective, real, and supratemporal in its significance.

V

Our result so far is that man indeed uses his ideas as means of controlling his experience, and that truth involves such control, but that truth cannot be defined solely in terms of our personal experience of our own success in obtaining this control.

Hereupon the second of the motives which we have found influencing the recent theories of truth comes to our aid. If instrumentalism needs a supplement, where are we, the individual thinkers, to look for that supplement, except in those inner personal grounds which incline each of us to make his own best interpretation of life precisely as he can, in accordance with his own will to succeed, and in accordance with his individual needs?

To be sure, as one may still insist, we are always dealing with live human experience, and with its endless constraints and limitations. And when we accept or reject opinions, we do so because, at the time, these opinions seem to us to promise a future empirical "working," a successful "control" over experience, — in brief, a success such as appeals to live human beings. Instrumentalism in so far correctly defines the nature which truth possesses in so far as we ever actually verify truth. And of course we always believe as we do because we are subject to the constraint of our present experience. But since we are social beings, and beings with countless and varied intelligent needs, we constantly define and accept as valid very numerous ideas and opinions whose truth we do not hope personally to verify. Our act in accepting such unverified truths is (as Professor James states the case) essentially similar to the act of the banker in accepting credit values instead of cash. A note or other evidence of value is good if it *can* be turned into cash at some agreed time, or under specified conditions. Just so, an idea is true, not merely at the moment when it enables somebody to control his own experience. It is true if, under definable conditions which, as a fact, you or I may never verify, it *would* enable some human being whose purposes agree with ours to control his own experience. If we personally do not verify a given idea, we can still accept it then upon its credit value. We can accept it precisely as paper, which cannot now be cashed, is accepted by one who regards that paper as, for a given purpose, or to a given extent, equivalent to cash. A bond, issued by a government, may promise payment after fifty years. The banker may to-day accept such a bond as good, and may pay cash for it, although he feels sure that he personally will never live to see the principal repaid by the borrower.

Now, as Professor James would say, it is in this sense that our ideas about past time, and about the content of other men's minds, and about the vast physical world, "with all its stars and milky ways," are accepted as true. Such ideas have for us credit values. We accept these ideas as true because we need to trade on credits. Borrowed truth is as valuable in the spiritual realm as borrowed money is in the commercial realm. To believe a now unverified truth is simply to say: "I accept that idea, upon credit, as equivalent to the cash payments in terms of live experience which, as I assert, I could get in case I had the opportunity."

And so much it is indeed easy to make out about countless assertions which we all accept. They are assertions about experience, but not about our present experience. They are made under various constraints of convention, habit, desire, and private conviction, but they are opinions whose truth is for us dependent upon our personal assent and acquiescence.

Herewith, however, we face what is, for more than one modern theory of truth, a very critical question. Apparently it is one thing to say: "I accept this opinion upon credit," and quite another thing to say: "The truth of this opinion consists, solely and essentially, in the fact that it is credited by me." In seeming, at least, it is one thing to assert: "We trade upon credit; we deal in credits," and quite another thing to say: "There is no value behind this bond or behind this bit of irredeemable paper currency, except its credit value." But perhaps a modern theory of truth may decline to accept such a difference as ultimate. Perhaps this theory may say: The truth *is* the credit. As a fact, a vast number of our human opinions — those, for instance, which relate to the past, or to the contents of other men's minds — appear, within the range of our personal experience, as credits whose value we, who believe the opinions, cannot hope ever to convert into the cash of experience. The banker who holds the bond not maturing within his own lifetime can, after all, if the bond is good, sell it to-day for cash. And that truth which he can personally and empirically test whenever he wants to test, is enough to warrant his act in accepting the credit. But I, who am confident of the truths of history, or of geology, or of physics, and who believe in the minds of other men, — I accept as valid countless opinions that are for me, in my private capacity and from an empirical point of view, nothing but irredeemable currency. In vain do I say: "I *could* convert these ideas into the cash of experience *if* I were some other man, or *if* I were living centuries ago instead of to-day." For the question simply recurs: In what sense are these propositions about my own possible experience true when I do not test their truth, — yes, true although I, personally, *cannot* test their truth? These credits, irredeemable in terms of the cash of my experience, — wherein consists their true credit value?

Here one apparently stands at the parting of the ways. One can answer this question by saying: "The truth of these assertions (or their falsity, if they are false) belongs to them whether I credit them or no, whether I verify them or not. Their truth or their falsity is their own character and is independent of my credit and my verification." But to say this appears to be, after all, just the intellectualism which so many of our modern pragmatists condemn. There remains, however, one other way. One can say: "The truth of the unverified assertions *consists simply in the fact that,* for our own private and individual ends, *they are credited.* Credit is relative to the creditor. If he finds that, on the whole, it meets his purpose to credit, he credits. And there is no truth, apart from present verifications, except this truth of credit." In other words, that is true for me which I find myself accepting as my way of reacting to my situation.

This, I say, is a theory of truth which can be attempted. Consider what a magnificent freedom such a theory gives to all of us. Credit is relative to the creditor. To be sure, if ever the day of reckoning should come, one would be subject, at the moment of verification, to the constraints of experience. At such times, one would either get the cash or would not get it. But after all very few of our ideas about this great and wonderful world of ours ever are submitted to any such sharp tests. History and the minds of other men, — well, our personal opinions about these remain credits that no individual amongst us can ever test for himself. As your world is mainly made up of such things, your view of your world remains, then, subject to your own needs. It ought to be thus subject. There is no absolute truth. There is only the truth that you need. Enter into the possession of your spiritual right. Borrow Nietzsche's phraseology. Call the truth of ordinary intellectualism mere *Sklavenwahrheit*. It pretends to be absolute; but only the slaves believe in it. "Henceforth," so some Zarathustra of a new theory of truth may say, "I teach you *Herrenwahrheit*." Credit what you choose to credit. Truth is made for man, not man for truth. Let your life "boil over" into new truth as much as you find such effervescence convenient. When, apart from the constraints of present verification, and apart from mere convention, I say: "This opinion of mine is true," I mean simply: "To my mind, lord over its own needs, this assertion now appears expedient." Whenever my expediency changes, my truth will change.

But does anybody to-day hold just *this* theory of truth? I hesitate to make accusations which some of my nearest and dearest friends may repudiate as personally injurious. But this I can say: I find a great many recent theorists about truth talking in just this spirit so long as they feel free to glorify their spiritual liberty, to amuse their readers with clever assaults upon absolutism, and to arouse sympathy by insistence upon the human and the democratic attractiveness of the novel views of truth that they have to advance. Such individualism, such capriciousness, is in the air. Our modern theorists of truth frequently speak in this way. When their expressions of such views are criticized, they usually modify and perhaps withdraw them. What, as individuals, such teachers really mean, I have no right to say. Nobody but themselves can say; and some of them seem to say whatever they please. But this I know: Whoever identifies the truth of an assertion with his own individual interest in making that assertion may be left to bite the dust of his own confusion in his own way and time. The outcome of such essential waywardness is not something that you need try to determine through controversy. It is self-determined. For in case I say to you: "The sole ground for my assertions is this, that I please to make them," — well, at once I am defining exactly the attitude which we all alike regard as the attitude of one who chooses *not* to tell the truth. And if, hereupon, I found a theory of truth upon generalizing such an assertion, — well, I am defining as truth-telling precisely that well-known practical attitude which is the contradictory of the truth-telling attitude. The contrast is not one between intellectualism and pragmatism. It is the contrast between two well-known attitudes of will, — the will that is loyal to truth as an universal ideal, and the will that is concerned with its own passing caprices. If I talk of truth, I refer to what the truth-loving sort of will seeks. If hereupon I define the true as that which the individual personally views as expedient in opinion or in assertion, I contradict myself, and may be left to my own confutation. For the position in which I put myself, by this individualistic theory of truth, is closely analogous to the position in which Epimenides the Cretan, the hero of the fallacy of the liar, was placed by his own so famous thesis.

VI

And yet, despite all this, the modern assault upon mere intellectualism is well founded. The truth of our assertions is indeed definable only by taking account of the meaning of our own individual attitudes of will, and the truth, whatever else it is, is at least instrumental in helping us towards the goal of all human volition. The only question is whether the will really means to aim at doing something that has a final and eternal meaning.

THE PROBLEM OF TRUTH

Herewith I suggest a theory of truth which we can understand only in case we follow the expressions of the third of the three modern motives to which I have referred. I have said that the new logic and the new methods of reasoning in the exact sciences are just now bringing us to a novel comprehension of our relation to absolute truth. I must attempt a very brief indication as to how this is indeed the case.

I have myself long since maintained that there is indeed a logic of the will, just as truly as there is a logic of the intellect. Personally, I go further still. I assert: all logic is the logic of the will. There is no pure intellect. Thought is a mode of action, a mode of action distinguished from other modes mainly by its internal clearness of self-consciousness, by its relatively free control of its own procedure, and by the universality, the impersonal fairness and obviousness of its aims and of its motives. An idea in the consciousness of a thinker is simply a present consciousness of some expression of purpose, — a plan of action.

A judgment is an act of a reflective and self-conscious character, an act whereby one accepts or rejects an idea as a sufficient expression of the very purpose that is each time in question. Our whole objective world is meanwhile defined for each of us in terms of our ideas. General assertions about the meaning of our ideas are reflective acts whereby we acknowledge and accept certain ruling principles of action. And in respect of all these aspects of doctrine I find myself at one with recent voluntarism, whether the latter takes the form of instrumentalism, or insists upon some more individualistic theory of truth. But for my part, in spite, or in fact because of this my voluntarism, I cannot rest in any mere relativism. Individualism is right in saying, "I will to credit this or that opinion." But individualism is wrong in supposing that I can ever be content with my own will in as far as it is merely an individual will. The will to my mind is to all of us nothing but a thirst for complete and conscious self-possession, for fullness of life. And in terms of this its central motive, the will defines the truth that it endlessly seeks as a truth that possesses completeness, totality, self-possession, and therefore absoluteness. The fact that, in our human experience, we never meet with any truths such as completely satisfy our longing for insight, this fact we therefore inevitably interpret, not as any defect in the truth, but as a defect in our present state of knowledge, a limitation due to our present type of individuality. Hence we acknowledge a truth which transcends our individual life. Our concepts of the objectively real world, our ethical ideals of conduct, our estimates of what constitutes the genuine worth of life, — all these constructions of ours are therefore determined by the purpose to conform our selves to absolute standards. We will the eternal. We define the eternal. And this we do whenever we talk of what we call genuine facts or actualities, or of the historical content of human experience, or of the physical world that our sciences investigate. If we try to escape this inner necessity of our whole voluntary and self-conscious life, we simply contradict ourselves. We can define the truth even of relativism only by asserting that relativism is after all absolutely true. We can admit our ignorance of truth only by acknowledging the absoluteness of that truth of which we are ignorant. And all this is no caprice of ours. All this results from a certain necessary nature of our will which we can test as often as we please by means of the experiment of trying to get rid of the postulate of an absolute truth. We shall find that, however often we try this experiment, the denial that there is any absolute truth simply leads to its own denial, and reinstates what it denies.

The reference that I a little while since made to our assertions regarding the past, and regarding the minds of other men, has already suggested to us how stubbornly we all assert certain truths which, for every one of us, transcend empirical verification, but which we none the less regard as absolutely true. If I say: "There never was a past," I contradict myself, since I assume the past even in asserting that a past never was. As a fact our whole interpretation of our experience is determined, in a sense akin to that which Kant defined, by certain modes of our own activity, whose significance is transcendental, even while their whole application is empirical. These modes of our activity make all our empirical sciences logically possible. Meanwhile it need not surprise us to find that Kant's method of defining these modes of our activity was not adequate, and that a new logic is giving us, in this field, new light. The true nature of these necessary modes of our activity becomes most readily observable to us in case we rightly analyze the methods and concepts, not of our own empirical, but rather of our mathematical sciences. For in these sciences our will finds its freest expression. And yet for that very reason in these sciences the absoluteness of the truth which the will defines is most obvious. The new logic to which I refer is especially a study of the logic of mathematics.

VII

That there are absolutely true propositions, the existence of the science of pure mathematics proves. It is indeed the case that, as Russell insists, the propositions of pure mathematics are (at least in general) hypothetical propositions. But the hypothetical character of the propositions of pure mathematics does not make the truth that a certain mathematically interesting consequent follows from a certain antecedent, in any way less than absolutely true. The assertion, "a implies b," where a and b are propositions, may be an absolutely true assertion; and, as a fact, the hypothetical assertions of pure mathematics possess this absolutely true character. Now it is precisely the nature and ground of this absoluteness of purely mathematical truth upon which recent research seems to me to have thrown a novel light. And the light which has appeared in this region seems to me to be destined to reflect itself anew upon all regions and types of truth, so that empirical and contingent, and historical and psychological and ethical truth, different as such other types of truth may be from mathematical truth, will nevertheless be better understood, in future, in the light of the newer researches into the logic of pure mathematics. I can only indicate, in the most general way, the considerations which I here have in mind.

At the basis of every mathematical theory, — as, for instance, at the basis of pure geometry, or pure number theory, — one finds a set of fundamental concepts, the so-called "indefinables" of the theory in question, and a set of fundamental "propositions," the so-called "axioms" of this theory. Modern study of the logic of pure mathematics has set in a decidedly novel light the question: What is the rational source, and what is the logical basis of these primal concepts and of these primal propositions of mathematical theory? I have no time here to deal with the complications of the recent discussion of this question. But so much I can at once point out: there are certain concepts and certain propositions which possess the character of constituting the doctrine which may be called, in the modern sense, Pure Logic. Some of these concepts and propositions were long ago noted by Aristotle. But the Aristotelian logic actually took account of only a portion of the concepts of pure logic, and was able to give, of these concepts, only a very insufficient analysis. There is a similar inadequacy about the much later analysis of the presuppositions of logic which Kant attempted. The theory of the categories is in fact undergoing, at present, a very important process of reconstruction. And this process is possible just because we have at present discovered wholly new means of analyzing the concepts and propositions in question. I refer (as I may in passing state) to the means supplied by modern Symbolic Logic.

Well, the concepts of pure logic, when once defined, constitute an inexhaustible source for the constructions and theories of pure mathematics. A set of concepts and of propositions such as can be made the basis of a mathematical theory is a set possessing a genuine and unquestionable significance if, and only if, these concepts and these propositions can be brought into a certain definite relation with the concepts and propositions of pure logic. This relation may be expressed by saying that if the conditions of general logical theory are such as to imply the valid possibility of the mathematical definitions and constructions in question, then — but only then — are the corresponding mathematical theories at once absolutely valid and significant. In brief, pure mathematics consists of constructions and theories based wholly upon the conceptions and propositions of pure logic.

The question as to the absoluteness of mathematical truth hereupon reduces itself to the question as to the absoluteness of the truths of pure logic.

Wherein, however, consists this truth of pure logic? I answer, at once, in my own way. Pure logic is the theory of the mere form of thinking. But what is thinking?

IN THE LIGHT OF DISCUSSION

Thinking, I repeat, is simply our activity of willing precisely in so far as we are clearly conscious of what we do and why we do it. And thinking is found by us to possess an absolute form precisely in so far as we find that there are certain aspects of our activity which sustain themselves even in and through the very effort to inhibit them. One who says: "I do not admit that for me there is any difference between saying yes and saying no," — says "no," and distinguishes negation from affirmation, even in the very act of denying this distinction. Well, affirmation and negation are such self-sustaining forms of our will activity and of our thought activity. And such self-sustaining forms of activity determine absolute truths. For instance, it is an absolute truth that there is a determinate difference between the assertion and the denial of a given proposition, and between the doing and the not doing of a given deed. Such absolute truths may appear trivial enough. Modern logical theory is for the first time making clear to us how endlessly wealthy in consequences such seemingly trivial assertions are.

The absoluteness of the truths of pure logic is shown through the fact that you can test these logical truths in this reflective way. They are truths such that to deny them is simply to reassert them under a new form. I fully agree, for my own part, that absolute truths are known to us only in such cases as those which can be tested in this way. I contend only that recent logical analysis has given to us a wholly new insight as to the fruitfulness of such truths.

VIII

An ancient example of a use of that way of testing the absoluteness of truth which is here in question is furnished by a famous proof which Euclid gave of the theorem, according to which there exists no last prime number in the ordinal sequence of the whole numbers. Euclid, namely, proved this theorem by what I suppose to be one device whereby individual instances of absolute truths are accessible to us men. He proved the theorem by showing that the denial of the theorem implies the truth of the theorem. That is, if I suppose that there is a last prime number, I even thereby provide myself with the means of constructing a prime number, which comes later in the series of whole numbers than the supposed "last" prime, and which certainly exists just as truly as the whole numbers themselves exist. Here, then, is one classic instance of an absolute truth.

To be sure Euclid's theorem about the prime numbers is a hypothetical proposition. It depends upon certain concepts and propositions about the whole numbers. But the equally absolute truth that the whole numbers themselves form an endless series, with no last term, has been subjected, in recent times, to wholly new forms of reëxamination by Dedekind, by Frege, and by Russell. The various methods used by these different writers involve substantially the same sort of consideration as that which Euclid already applied to the prime numbers. There are certain truths which you cannot deny without denying the truth of the first principles of pure logic. But to deny these latter principles is to reassert them under some other and equivalent form. Such is the common principle at the basis of the recent reëxamination of the concept of the whole numbers. Dedekind, in showing that the existence of the dense ordinal series of the rational numbers implies the existence of the Dedekind *Schnitte* of this series, discovered still another absolute, although of course hypothetical, truth which itself implies the truth of the whole theory of the so-called real numbers. Now all such discoveries are indeed revelations of absolute truth in precisely this sense, that at the basis of all the concepts and propositions about number there are concepts and propositions belonging to pure logic; while if you deny these propositions of pure logic, you imply, by this very denial, the reassertion of what you deny. To discover this fact, to see that the denial of a given proposition implies the reassertion of that proposition, is not, as Kant supposed, something that you can accomplish, if at all, then only by a process of mere "analysis." On the contrary, Euclid's proof as to the prime numbers, and the modern exact proofs of the fundamental theorems of mathematics, involve, in general, a very difficult synthetic process, — a construction which is by no means at first easy to follow. And the same highly synthetic constructions run through the whole of modern logic.

Now once again what does one discover when he finds out such absolute truths? I do not believe, as Russell believes, that one in such cases discovers truths which are simply and wholly independent of our constructive processes. On the contrary, what one discovers is distinctly what I must call a voluntaristic truth, — a truth about the creative will that thinks the *truth*. One discovers, namely, that our constructive processes, viewed just as activities, possess a certain absolute nature and conform to their own self-determined but, for that very reason, absolute laws. One finds out in such cases what one must still, with absolute necessity, do under the presupposition that one is no longer bound by the constraints of ordinary experience, but is free, as one is in pure mathematics free, to construct whatever one can construct. The more, in such cases, one deals with what indeed appear to be, in one aspect, "*freie Schöpfungen des menschlichen Geistes,*" the more one discovers that their laws, which are the fundamental and immanent laws of the will itself, are absolute. For one finds what it is that one must construct even if one denies that, in the ideal world of free construction which one is seeking to define, that construction has a place. In brief, all such researches illustrate the fact that while the truth which we acknowledge is indeed relative to the will which acknowledges that truth, still what one may call the pure form of willing is an absolute form, a form which sustains itself in the very effort to violate its own laws. We thus find out absolute truth, but it is absolute truth about the nature of the creative will in terms of which we conceive all truths.

Now it is perfectly true that such absolute truth is not accessible to us in the empirical world, in so far as we deal with individual phenomena. But it is also true that we all of us conceive the unity of the world of experience — the meaning, the sense, the connection of its facts — in terms of those categories which express precisely this very form of our creative activity. Hence, although every empirical truth is relative, all relative truth is inevitably defined by us as subject to conditions which themselves are absolute. This, which Kant long ago maintained, gets a very new meaning in the light of recent logic, — a far deeper meaning, I think, than Kant could conceive.

In any case, the new logic, and the new mathematics, are making us acquainted with absolute truth, and are giving to our knowledge of this truth a clearness never before accessible to human thinking. And yet the new logic is doing all this in a way that to my mind is in no wise a justification of the intellectualism which the modern instrumentalists condemn. For what we hereby learn is that all truth is indeed relative to the expression of our will, but that the will inevitably determines for itself forms of activity which are objectively valid and absolute, just because to attempt to inhibit these forms is once more to act, and is to act in accordance with them. These forms are the categories both of our thought and of our action. We recognize them equally whether we consider, as in ethics, the nature of reasonable conduct, or, as in logic, the forms of conceptual construction, or, as in mathematics, the ideal types of objects that we can define by constructing, as freely as possible, in conformity with these forms. When we turn back to the world of experience, we inevitably conceive the objects of experience in terms of our categories. Hence the unity and the transindividual character which rightly we assign to the objects of experience. What we know about these objects is always relative to our human needs and activities. But all of this relative knowledge is — however provisionally — defined in terms of absolute principles. And that is why the scientific spirit and the scientific conscience are indeed the expression of motives, which you can never reduce to mere instrumentalism, and can never express in terms of any individualism. And that is why, wherever two or three are gathered together in any serious moral or scientific enterprise, they believe in a truth which is far more than the mere working of any man's ephemeral assertions.

In sum, an absolute truth is one whose denial implies the reassertion of that same truth. To us men, such truths are accessible only in the realm of our knowledge of the forms that predetermine all of our concrete activities. Such knowledge we can obtain regarding the categories of pure logic and also regarding the constructions of pure mathematics. In dealing, on the other hand, with the concrete objects of experience, we are what the instrumentalists suppose us to be, namely, seekers for a successful control over this experience. And as the voluntarists also correctly emphasize, in all our empirical constructions, scientific and practical, we express our own individual wills and seek such success as we can get. But there remains the fact that in all these constructions we are expressing a will which, as logic and pure mathematics teach us, has an universal absolute nature, — the same in all of us. And it is for the sake of winning some adequate expression of this our absolute nature, that we are constantly striving in our empirical world for a success which we never can obtain at any instant, and can never adequately define in any merely relative terms. The result appears in our ethical search for absolute standards, and in our metaphysical thirst for an absolute interpretation of the universe, — a thirst as unquenchable as the over-individual will that expresses itself through all our individual activities is itself world-wide, active, and in its essence absolute.

In recognizing that all truth is relative to the will, the three motives of the modern theories of truth are at one. To my mind they, therefore, need not remain opposed motives. Let us observe their deeper harmony, and bring them into synthesis. And then what I have called the trivialities of mere instrumentalism will appear as what they are, — fragmentary hints, and transient expressions, of that will whose life is universal, whose form is absolute, and whose laws are at once those of logic, of ethics, of the unity of experience, and of whatever gives sense to life.

Tennyson, in a well-known passage of his "In Memoriam," cries:

> "Oh living Will that shalt endure
> When all that seems shall suffer shock,
> Rise in the spiritual rock,
> Flow through our deeds and make them pure."

That cry of the poet was an expression of moral and religious sentiment and aspiration; but he might have said essentially the same thing if he had chosen the form of praying: Make our deeds logical. Give our thoughts sense and unity. Give our Instrumentalism some serious unity of eternal purpose. Make our Pragmatism more than the mere passing froth of waves that break upon the beach of triviality. In any case, the poet's cry is an expression of that Absolute Pragmatism, of that Voluntarism, which recognizes all truth as the essentially eternal creation of the Will. What the poet utters is that form of Idealism which seems to me to be indicated as the common outcome of all the three motives that underlie the modern theory of truth.

ESSAY V

IMMORTALITY

ESSAY V

IMMORTALITY [1]

ALL questions about Immortality relate to some form of the continuance of human life in time, beyond death. All such questions presuppose, then, the conception of time. But now, what is Time? How is it related to Truth, to Reality, to God? And if any answer to these questions can be suggested, what light do such answers throw on man's relation to time, and on the place of death in the order of time?

Secondly, all questions about Immortality relate to the survival of human personality. But, what is our human personality? What aspect of a man do you want to have survive? In considering these two sets of questions, I shall be led to mention in passing several others, all of which bear upon our topic.

[1] An address prepared for an Association of Clergymen in March, 1906.

IMMORTALITY

My honored colleague, Professor Münsterberg, in his recent little book on "The Eternal Life," has raised in a somewhat novel form an old issue regarding the metaphysics of time, and has applied his resulting opinion to our problem of immortality. The real world, he has said, — the world of the absolute, — is an essentially timeless world — a world of meanings, of ideal values — a world where there is no question of how long things endure, but only a question as to what value they have in the whole of real life. In this genuinely real world of ideal values everything has eternal being in accordance with its absolute worth. A value cannot be lost, for it belongs to the timeless whole. But the ordinary point of view, which so emphasizes time, as most of us do, is merely a quantitative view — a falsification, or at least a narrowing, of the truth — a transformation of reality — a translation of its meaning into the abstract terms of a special set of concepts — concepts useful in our human science and in our daily business, but not valid for the student of real life. Matter, indeed, endures in time; but then matter is a conceptual entity, a phenomenon, a creation, of the scientific point of view. A man endures in time while his body lives; but this is only the man as viewed in relation to the clocks and to the calendars — the phenomenal man — the man of the street and the market place, of the psychological laboratory and of the scientific record, of the insurance agents and of the newspapers. The real man whom you estimate and love is not this phenomenal man in time, but the man of will and of meaning, of ideals and of personal character, whose value you acknowledge. This real man is — what he is worth. His place in the world is determined not by the time during which he endures, but by the moral values which he expresses, and which the Absolute timelessly recognizes for what they eternally are. This real man does not come and go. He is. To say that he is immortal is merely to say that he has timeless value. And to say that is to express your love for him in its true meaning.

Hence, as Professor Münsterberg holds,

IMMORTALITY

the whole problem about immortality is falsely stated in popular discussion. Revise your view of time. See how time is but an appearance belonging to the world of description; that is, the world of conceptual clocks and calendars; and then the real man is known to you, not as temporally outlasting death, but as, in his timeless ethical value, in the real world of appreciation, deathless. For he belongs to the realm of meanings; and the timeless Absolute of real life neither waits for him to come, nor misses him after his death as one passed away, but acknowledges him in his true value as what he is, the real person, whose eternal significance as little requires his endless endurance in the unreal conceptual time of the calendar and of the clock makers, as this same significance requires him to have a taller stature than he has in the equally unreal conceptual space of the metric system and of the tailor's measuring tape.

So far my colleague, as I venture to restate his view. I do not agree with him in the way in which he has formulated and applied this view. Yet I think that Professor Münsterberg is at least in one respect justified in printing his essay. He is justified, namely, in calling our attention to the fact that, in order to discuss immortality exhaustively, we must include in our discussion some view of the sense in which time itself is a reality. And I also think that my colleague's view of time, although not mine, contains an important element of truth. Let me try to suggest what this element is.

I need not say to theologically trained readers that you cannot well conceive of God without supposing the Divine Being to be otherwise related to time than we men just now are. To view the Deity as just now waiting, as we wait, for the vicissitudes of coming experience that are floating down the time stream towards him, to conceive the divine foreknowledge merely as a sort of clever computation of what will yet happen, a neat prediction of the fortunes that God has yet to expect — well, I cannot suppose any competent theologian to be satisfied thus to conceive of the divine knowledge of time, or of what time contains. If God is merely the potent computer and predicter, whose expectations as to the future have never yet been disappointed, then he remains merely upon the level of a mighty fortune teller and fortune controller — a magician after all. And not thus can you be content to conceive of the divine omniscience. If the question arose: Why might not God's foreknowledge some day prove to have been fallible? Why might not revolving time force upon him unexpected facts? — then you would certainly reply: "If God, as God, absolutely foreknows, that means, properly viewed, not merely that he skillfully anticipates, or even that he mightily controls fortune, but that time, present, past, future, is somehow his own, is somehow at once for him, is an eternal present for which he has not to wait, a total expression of his will which he not merely remembers or anticipates, but views in one whole, *totum simul*, as St. Thomas well insisted."

God's relation to time cannot, then, be

merely our own present human relation. We expect what is not yet. But if God is God, he views the future and the past as we do the present. And in so far Professor Münsterberg's view is indeed well founded. The lasting or the passing away of things as we view them does not express the whole divine view of them. What has, for us men, passed away, is, for the divine omniscience, not lost. What is future is, from the divine point of view, a presentation. Time is in God, rather than is God in time. Some such view you surely must take if God is to be conceived at all.

But if God views facts as they are, this indeed implies that death, and the passing away of man, and the lapse of countless lives into what we call the forgotten past, cannot really be what we take these things to be — an absolutely real loss to reality of values which, but for death, would not become thus unreal. As a fact, I do not doubt that the least fact of transient experience has a meaning for the divine point of view — a meaning which we very ill express when we say of such a fact:

IMMORTALITY

"It passes, it is done, it is no more." In reality — that is, from the divine point of view — there can be no absolute loss of what is once to be viewed as real at all.

Now so far, using, to be sure, for the moment, theological rather than my colleague's metaphysical terms, I suggest a view about time which is obviously close to that which Professor Münsterberg emphasizes. Nevertheless I do not agree with him that, by means of such considerations, we can completely define the sense in which man is immortal. I turn, then, from this first naturally vague effort to hint that our human view of time is inadequate, and that even our present brief lives have a divine meaning which no human view of their transiency exhausts, — I turn, I say, from this glance into general theology, back to the problem about time, as we men have to conceive time. We talk of to-morrow, of the time after death, of the future in general. In that future, we say, we are to live or not to live. Every such formula, every such hypothesis, presupposes some sense in which our words about the future can have truth, even to-day — presupposes then some doctrine about what time is, and about how the past and future are related to the present. We must therefore ask again, but now in a more definite way, What reality has time, whether for the universe or for us?

It requires but little reflection to see that, in our ordinary speech about time, we are accustomed to use obscure, if not contradictory, language. We often ascribe true reality to the present only, and speak as if the past, as being over and done with, had no reality whatever; while the future, as yet unborn, we hereupon view as if it were also wholly unreal. The present, however, — this only real region of time, — we often speak of that as a mere point, having no duration whatever. Yet in this point we place all reality; and meanwhile, even as we name it, this sole reality vanishes and becomes past. Time, however, if thus defined, consists of two unreal regions, which contain together all duration — all that ever has been or will be; and time, in addition to these, its unreal halves, contains just one real instant, which itself has no duration, and which is thus no extended part of time at all, but only a vanishing presence. Thus, after all, there remains, when thus viewed, no real region in time at all. Nothing is; all crumbles. Such a view has only to be explicitly stated in order to be recognized as inadequate; as a fact, such a view is a mere heap of false abstractions. Moreover, we ourselves not only frequently assert, but almost as constantly deny, this interpretation of time. For the past we view, after all, as a very stern and hard reality. What is done, is done. The past is irrevocable, unchangeable, adamantine, the safest of storehouses, the home of the eternal ages. Moreover, you can tell the truth about the past. Hence the past is surely not unreal in the sense in which fairyland is unreal. A man who practically treats the past as unreal, becomes *ipso facto* a liar; and you might in fact define a false witness as a man who tries to make the past over at will, not recognizing its stern and

IMMORTALITY

unalterable truth. On the other hand, the future indeed is not thus irrevocable; but it has its own sort of very potent and recognizable being. You constantly live by adjusting yourself to the reality of the future. The coal strike threatens. You wish that your coal bins, if they are not full, were full. For next winter, after all, is a reality. Thus, then, the two regions of time, the past and future, are not wholly unreal. For the truthful witness the past is a reality. For the faithful maker of promises the future is a reality. As for the present, — after all, are many dreams less real than is the *mere* present? Fools live in the present, and dream there, taking it to be the real world. But whoever acts wisely, knows that the present is merely his chance for a deed; and that the worth of a deed is determined by its intended relations to past and future. Not the present, then, of our flickering human consciousness, is the temporal reality, so much as are the past and the future. Life has its dignity through its bearing upon their contents and their meaning.

IMMORTALITY

We see from these illustrations, I hope, that much of our common speech about time is belied by our practical attitudes towards time. Truthful reports and promises, serious deeds and ideals, prudence and conservatism and enterprise, all unite to show us that the reality of time is possessed especially by its past and its future, over against which the present is indeed but vanishing. And now what, after all, do such illustrations teach us regarding the true meaning of our conception of time?

I answer at once, dogmatically, — but, as I hope, not without some suggestion of the reason for my answer: Time, to my mind, is an essential practical aspect of reality, which derives its whole meaning from the nature and from the life of the will. Take away from your conception of the world the idea of a being who has a will, who has a practical relation to facts; take away the idea of a being who looks before and after, who strives, seeks, hopes, pursues, records, reports, promises, accomplishes; take away, I say, every idea of such a being from your world, and whatever then remains in your conceived world gives you no right to a conception of time as any real aspect of things. The time of the timepieces and of mechanical science, the time of geology and of physics, is indeed, as Professor Münsterberg maintains, but an abstraction. This abstraction is useful in the natural sciences. But it has no ultimate meaning except in relation to beings that have a will, that live a practical life, and that mean to do something. Given such beings, it can be shown that they need the conception of the time of mechanics or of geology in order to define their relation to nature. But apart from their needs, time is nothing. The time regions, already mentioned in this account, get their distinct types of reality solely from their diverse relations to a finite will, and, for us, to our own finite will. The past is that portion of reality where, to be sure, deeds also belong; but these past deeds are presupposed by my present attitude of will as already, and irrevocably, accomplished facts. As such they

IMMORTALITY

are the acknowledged basis upon which all present deeds rest. That is, then, what I mean by the past, viz. the presupposed and hence irrevocable basis on which my present deed rests. I say, "So much is done." The will, therefore, presupposing the past, asks, "What next?" and is ready to decide by further action. The future is equally definable solely in terms of the will. The future is the region of the opportunity of the finite will. The future also, indeed, contains its aspect of destiny — as, for example, next winter's chill. But it likewise contains the chance of deeds yet undone, and so incites the will. As for the present, it is the scintillating flash of the instant's opportunity and accomplishment. It too is meaningless except for the deed, be this deed a mere act of attention or an outward expression. In terms, then, of my attitude of will, and only in such terms, can I define time, and its regions, distinctions, and reality.

Time then is, I should say, a peculiarly obvious instance of the necessity for defining

IMMORTALITY

the universe in idealistic terms — that is, in terms of life, of will, of conscious meaning. Burdened as we all are by the mere concept of the time of the clock makers and of the calendars, by the equally conceptual time of theoretical physics and of daily business, we are prone to forget that it is the human will itself which defines for us all such concepts, which abstracts them from life, and which then often bows to them as if they were indeed mere fate. If you look beneath the abstractions, you find that time is in essence the form of the finite will, and that when I acknowledge one universal world time, I do so only by extending the conception of the will to the whole world. If I say: "There is to come a future," I mean merely: My will acknowledges deeds yet to be done, and defines as the future reality of the universe a will continuous with my will — a world will in whose expression my present deed has its place. The unity and continuity of the time of the universe are definable only through the practical relation of my will to this world will. My deed has its place in the system of the world's deeds. The will that is yet to be expressed in the future is inseparable in its essence from the will which even now, and in my present deed, acknowledges this future as its own. As appears from these forms of expression, I am in philosophy an idealist. This is no place to set forth lengthy arguments for idealism. I have to sketch and to speak dogmatically. But the conception of time is peculiarly good as an illustration of the need of idealism.

My result is, so far, that time is indeed indefinable and meaningless except as the form in which a conscious will process expresses its own coherent series of deeds and of meanings. And so, if all the finite world is subject to one time process, this assertion means merely that all our wills are together partial expressions of a single conscious volitional process — the process whereby the world will gets expressed in finite forms and deeds. A complete argument for idealism would, of course, have to develop and to supplement this interpretation of time in many ways. But here is a hint of idealism.

IMMORTALITY

A result so stated is, I admit, not at first sight at all decisive as to any question of personal immortality. Yet I hope that the reader will already see how a doctrine of this sort, dogmatically as I have to state it, fragmentarily as I have to suggest my reasons for holding it, must have some bearing upon the problem as to how and whether a personal survival of death is a possibility. One is too much disposed to view the time process as an utterly foreign fate, physically forced upon unwilling mortals, who can only lament how youth flies, and how the good old times come again no more, and how the unknown future, vast and merciless, is impending and is yet to engulf us. What I now point out is that all such abstract conceptions of the fatal, external, physical, inhuman, unconscious reality of the world's time process are inadequate. As we have seen, in our sketch of a few such false conceptions, they appear in various, in paradoxically conflicting forms, which sometimes treat all time as unreal except the present, and sometimes view the past and future as

IMMORTALITY

an iron reality of blind fate. As a fact, so I insist, we concretely know time as the form of the will. We define the time relations practically, and in terms of deeds done and to be done. If we generalize our time experience, so as conceptually to view the whole world as expressing itself in a single temporal process, our generalization means this: that the entire world is the expression of a single will, which is in its totality continuous with our own, so that the past and future of our personal will is also the past and future of this world will, and conversely.

The lesson, however, is already this: If, as is very obviously true, there was a time when I personally did not exist, then that was because the world will did not then yet need, and so did not yet involve, in its own expression, and as a part thereof, my personal deeds. If, on the other hand, the time is to come when I, in my private personality, shall have become extinct, that can be only because the world will as a whole, after my passing away,

IMMORTALITY

is thenceforth to presuppose all of my personal deeds as irrevocably done, and is to have no longer any need to include my further choices. Assume, for the moment, that this is to be the case. This world will, however, is in any event not foreign in nature to my own will, but is continuous therewith; just as continuous, namely, as the real time of my own consciousness is continuous with the real time of the universe. If I die, then, and finally cease, that will be because a will — a conscious will — a will essentially continuous with my own — a will now expressed in my consciousness, but sure to be forever expressed in *some* consciousness — a will that now includes all my hopes and my meanings — must some day come to look back upon my personal life as an expression no longer needed. My extinction, then, if it comes, will be at all events a teleological, not a merely fatal process — an inner and purposive checking of the very will which now throbs in me — a checking which will also be a significant attainment — not a blind passing away, due to the mere fate that, in

IMMORTALITY

time, all becomes unreal. "Our life," said wondrous old Heraclitus, "is the death of gods; our death is the life of gods." And Heraclitus meant by these words that if indeed all passes away, and if we pass too, that can only be because that very divine life which now lives in us will, living in other divine forms, accomplish the very meaning which it now partially accomplishes in us, by expressing itself otherwise, and yet as the very life which is now ours. "For we are also his offspring."

Considerations such as these are indeed but highly fragmentary. They certainly do not by themselves give any adequate notion of immortality. They have been emphasized by many thinkers who thereby meant merely to make light of personal permanence. Nevertheless, to conceive time as the form of the will, and universal time as the form of the world will, and our lives as linked to a conscious world will by precisely as close a link as binds the time of our consciousness — to conceive of all this, I say, is to be helped to a sort of introduction to a more definite view of our problem. In time you are at any rate not lost as the snows are lost when they melt; or engulfed as the mountains are engulfed when they are washed away and sink, as sediment, into the sea. For the world time is also the time of your consciousness; and, in precisely as genuine a sense, the world will is your will. If you ever become extinct, that will occur only as a single deed, or as a partial expression, becomes extinct for the doer who, presupposing that very deed, bases his own further expression upon the acknowledgment, the valuation, and the memory of the past deed itself. The question whether such extinction will occur at all thus gets its proper teleological formulation. You will die, not as blind fate determines, nor merely because time flies: you will die, if at all, because the world will needs no more of your personal deeds, except in so far as they are henceforth merely presupposed.

So far, then, I suggest what might be called a voluntaristic theory of the time process.

IMMORTALITY

I understand, I may say, that Professor Münsterberg would in large measure agree with even this account of the time relations as due to, as expressions of, the significant attitudes of a world will. The point where my colleague and I are at variance is now ready for a clearer statement than is the one so far given in this discussion. The difference relates to the way in which this entire will process, this whole expression of significant activities in the universe, appears when viewed, so to speak, *sub specie eternitatis;* that is, in its wholeness, as God must be conceived to view it — or as any one ought to view it who does not confine himself to the abstract concepts of the clock makers and of the calendars, but who considers real life as it genuinely is, in its veritable meaning.

The time process is the form of the will. Past and future differ as deeds yet to be done differ from presupposed and irrevocable deeds. The present is the vanishing opportunity for the single deed. The time distinctions, then, are relative to deeds and to meanings. Grant all this for a moment. What follows? Does it follow that whoever views the world life as it truly is, sees the whole world as a timeless totality, consisting simply of meanings, of acts, of will attitudes, whose relations are not temporal, but significant? Does it follow that endurance in time is no test of the worth of a personality, any more than colossal stature is needed as an attribute of a great personality?

I cannot agree to such a conclusion, in the form in which Professor Münsterberg states it. First, then, as to the supposed timelessness of the world of real meanings, let me use an æsthetic example. Music, which Schopenhauer called an image of the will, is in any case essentially an art that expresses beautifully significant musical meanings in temporal order. Abstract, however, from the time form of music, and what is left of any musical form whatever? If the gods listen to music at all, they must appreciate its sequences. Wherein consists, however, a true musical appreciation? Whoever aimlessly half listens to the musical accompaniments of a dance or of a public festival, may indeed be so absorbed in the passing instant's sound that he gets no sense of the whole. True listening to music grasps, in a certain sense as a *totum simul*, entire sequences — measures, phrases, movements, symphonies. But such wiser listening and appreciation is not timeless. It does not ignore sequence. It is time-inclusive. It grasps as an entirety a sequence which transcends any one temporal present. In this grasping of the whole of a time process one gets a consciousness of a present which is no longer merely a vanishing present, but a time-including, a relatively eternal present, in which various vanishing instants have their places as relatively present, past, and future one to another.

Well, such a view, as I take it, comes nearer to getting the sense of what real life is than does any view which considers its world merely as timeless. If, then, I try to conceive how God views things, I can only suppose, not that the absolute view ignores time, but that the absolute view sees at a glance all time, past, present, future, just as the true appreciator of the music knows the entirety of the sequence as a sort of higher or inclusive present — a present in which the earlier stages do not merely vanish into the later stages, and yet, on the other hand, are not at all devoid of time relations to the later stages. For this inclusive view, as I suppose, sees the totality of the significant deeds and will attitudes as a single life process — temporal because it is both significant and volitional, — and present, not in the vanishing, but in the inclusive and eternal sense — present not as a timeless whole, but as an infinite sequence — "one undivided soul of many a soul," one life in infinite variety of expression.

For such a view, however, — a view which is not timeless, but time-inclusive — the duration of a given series of will acts, the wealth, the lasting, the variety of a distinguishable portion of the entire process, might have — yes, must have — a true relation to the degree of the significance which this portion of the whole possesses. A truly great work of musical art must involve a considerable sequence. Its length has a definable relation to its greatness. What is true of a work of art might be true of so much of the world life as constitutes an individual finite being. There might be significant time processes — individual lives, so to speak — whose meaning would require them to be endless, and whose place in the whole might demand that, once having appeared, they could never in the later will activities of the temporal order be ignored, but must thenceforth coöperate — the temporal will process always including amongst its deeds activities which were not only its own, but also their own.

If such individual lives, distinct in their meaning from other partial expressions of the world will, endless in their duration from some one point onwards, were actually factors in the world process, and were amongst the facts which the absolute view of real life had to include, in order to express and to find its own complete truth — how would such lives be related to the world life in its entirety? How would they be related to that absolute insight, to that divine view, which, in an eternal, that is, in a time-inclusive sense, would see at a glance the entirety of the world process?

If I try to suggest, however vaguely, an answer to these momentous questions, the reader will understand that I am merely sketching, and am not now trying to prove, what elsewhere I have discussed with tedious detail, and in a far more technical way. Here we have no time to weigh arguments pro and con. I can only outline, in a dogmatic way, my views. I merely suggest a few of their reasons.

I have spoken of a world will. I have said that to recognize, as we all do, one time process as holding for all the world, is to recognize the world will as a single volitional process in which all our lives are bound up. We are simply different modes of willing, continuously related to one another and to the total world will which throbs and strives in all of us alike, but which, in endless variety, seeks

IMMORTALITY

now this and now that special aim — accomplishes now this and now that special deed — presupposes an infinity of deeds as its own past — goes on to an infinity of deeds as its future — is content to be no one of us, but shows in our social life the community of our endlessly various aims, as in our individual lives it exhibits an endless variety of differentiations and of distinguishable trends of purpose. It is one will in us all; yet I have tried to show, elsewhere, that this does not deprive us of individuality. It needs our variety and our freedom. And we need its unity and its inexhaustible fertility of suggestion. We read the symbols of this inexhaustible fertility when we study nature, and when we commune with man. We acknowledge this unity whenever we view the time of the world as one time. Our own will to live is the will of the world, conscious in us, and demanding our individual variety as its own mode of expression. We conspire with the world will even when most we seem to rebel. We are one with it even when most we think of ourselves as separate. Art, ethics, reason, science, service, all bear witness both to our unity with its purposes, and to its need that all unity of purpose should be expressed through an endless variety of individual activities.

I have thus spoken of the world will as this infinitely complex unity in the variety of all finite wills. I have also spoken of an absolute point of view, which views this entire life of the world will as one whole. I have used theological speech, and have called this absolute point of view that of the divine being, the point of view of God. Now this is no opportunity to consider either the proofs for the divine existence or the problem regarding the nature of God. I have again to use dogmatic forms of speech. I mean by the term "God" the totality of the expressions and life of the world will, when considered in its conscious unity. God is a consciousness which knows and which intends the entire life of the world, a consciousness which views this life at one glance, as its own life and self, and which therefore not only wills but attains, not only seeks but possesses, not only passes from expression to expression, but eternally is the entire temporal sequence of its own expressions. God has and is a will, and this will, if viewed as a temporal sequence of activities, is identical with what I have called the world will. Only, when viewed as the divine will this world will is taken not merely as an infinite sequence of will activities, but in its eternal unity as one whole of life. God is omniscient, because his insight comprehends and finds unified, in one eternal instant, the totality of the temporal process, with all of its contents and meanings. He is omnipotent, because all that is done is, when viewed in its unity, his deed, and that despite the endless varieties and strifes which freedom and which the variety of individual finite expressions involve. God is immanent in the finite, because nothing is which is not a part of his total self-expression. He is transcendent of all finitude, because the totality of finite processes is before him at once, while nothing finite possesses true totality.

IMMORTALITY

If one hereupon asks, Why should there be finitude, variety, imperfection, temporal sequence at all? — we can only answer: Not otherwise can true and concrete perfection be expressed than through the overcoming of imperfections. Not otherwise can absolute attainment be won than through an infinite sequence of temporal strivings. Not otherwise can absolute personality exist than as mediated through the unification of the lives of imperfect and finite personalities. Not otherwise can the infinite live than through incarnation in finite form, and a rewinning of its total meaning through a conquest of its own finitude of expression. Not otherwise can rational satisfaction find a place than through a triumph over irrational dissatisfactions. The highest good logically demands a conquering of evil. The eternal needs expression in a temporal sequence whereof the eternal is the unity. The divine will must, as world will, differentiate itself into individuals, sequences, forms of finitude, into strivings, into ignorant seekings after the light, into doubting, erring, wandering beings, that even hereby the perfection of the spirit may be won. Perfect through suffering — this is the law of the divine perfection.

All these assertions would need, were there time, their own defense. I do not assert them as merely my own. That they are substantially true is what the whole lesson of the moral and religious experience of our race seems to me to have led us to see. That they are necessarily true can, as I think, be demonstrated.

So much, then, for some hint as to how the temporal is, to my mind, related to the eternal.

But what, one may ask, has all this to do with deciding the problem regarding immortality? Much, every way, I reply, if you only add, at this point, a little reflection as to the second of the two questions with which this paper opened. We have studied our relation to time, and also have considered the relation of time to the divine being. But what, so we asked at the outset, is a human personality?

Incidentally, as it were, we have now almost answered this question, so far as it here concerns us.

A human personality has many aspects, psychological, physical, social, ethical. But a man is a significant being by virtue not of his body, or his feelings, or his fortunes, or his social status, but by virtue of his will. The concept of personality is an ethical concept. A man, as an ethical being, is what he purposes to be, so far as his purpose is as yet temporally expressed. So far as his will is not yet expressed, his life belongs to the future. All else about him besides his will, his purpose, his life plan, his ideal, his deed, his volitional expression, — all else than this, I say, is mere material for manhood, mere clothing, mere environment, or mere fortune. Ignorantly as he now expresses himself, his worth lies not in the extent of his knowledge, but in the seriousness of his intent to express himself. Is he a sinner, then he is not yet true to his own will; that is, he is not yet, in the temporal order, his own complete and genuinely ideal self. For my duty is only my own will brought to a reasonable self-consciousness, and is not an external restraint. Hence the sinner is not yet his own explicit self. His conflict with the world is also an internal conflict — an inner war with his own imperfection. But if one who appears in the outer form of man shows no sign as yet of having any personal ideal, or life plan, or purpose, or individual will at all, then one can only say, "Since here we find a seemingly blind expression of the world will, but not an expression that as yet gives an account of itself, we must indeed suppose that some form of personality is here, in this fragment of the time process, latent, but we simply cannot tell what form." In such a case we indeed call the being whom we know in our human relations a person; but he so far appears as a person by courtesy. An explicit personality is one which shows itself through deeds that embody a coherent ideal — an ideal — an ideal which need not be abstractly formulated, but which must be practically active, recognizably significant, consciously in need of further temporal expression. Such an explicit personality may be that of a hero, of a saint, or of a rascal. The hero and the saint are simply personalities that are so far expressed in forms whose deeds and ideals have a truer internal harmony. A rascal is a finite personality who is, so far as his personality is yet expressed, essentially at war with himself, as he is with the world. For his deeds are opposed to his true meaning. In so far as he appears to us, as he often does, to be a contented rascal or a joyous sinner, who observes not this essential warfare with himself — in just so far, I say, he is a fool, and, accordingly, in just so far he lacks explicit personality; so that, when we judge him as such a joyous rascal, we know not with what personality we are dealing. But the awakened sinner, however obstinate in his wrong-doing, is a consciously tragic figure. He may also be much of a hero. We shall then admire his vigor. But he remains a warfare of ideals and deeds, and so is not yet come to himself. The true hero, the righteous man, the saint, — these are personalities on a higher level. But at no one point in time have they attained their total expression. For the dutiful will, in a finite being, is insatiable. It views itself as a dutiful will in so far as it seeks something yet to be done; and it views itself as an individual dutiful will in so far as it consciously says: "Since this is my duty, nobody else in the universe — no, not God, in so far as God is other than myself — can do this duty for me. My duty I must myself do. And wherever in time I stand, I am dissatisfied with what is so far done. I must pass on to the next."

Saints and sinners, so far as they are indeed explicit personalities, that is, finite wills conscious of their own individual intent, agree in being, in the temporal world, practically dissatisfied. The righteous man is dissatisfied with his present opportunity to express his will. He needs yet further future opportunities to do his duty. The conscious sinner is dissatisfied with the very will which he is at the moment trying to express. Each, as a finite being, engaged in a temporal process, is a person by virtue of his very "dissatisfactions." I refer now by the word "dissatisfaction," not to gloomy feelings, so much as to eagerness for further deeds. How we feel is a matter of fortune. How active we need to be, that constitutes our very selves, as now we are. For a finite personality, I insist, is a will to do something. So far as I have something yet to do, I am, however, dissatisfied with the past as with the present. I demand, in just so far, a future — a future in which, since I am now a sinner, at war with myself, I shall come into unity with my own will, and shall discover what it is that I am seeking — a future in which, in so far as even now I know and intend my duty, I shall further express this will of mine in the countless deeds that my personal purpose requires me yet to do.

So much, then, for a hint regarding what a finite personality is. But in view of all the foregoing, how shall we say that such a finite personality is related to the world and to God? I reply: A finite personality, as a conscious expression of the world will, is, when viewed in time, an expression of what is just now a dissatisfaction — and of a dissatisfaction of this very personality with itself. In so far as consciously sinful, this personality is dissatisfied with what it so far knows about its own will; but in so far as it is a finite doer of deeds, this personality, whether just or unjust, is dissatisfied with what it has so far done to express its will. Hence it looks to the future. And our very conception of the temporal future is due to this our present active dissatisfaction.

That such dissatisfactions should be at all in the world is due, however, as we have said, to that general need which demands that the eternal should be expressed through the temporal, that the divine and absolute should take on human and fallible form, and that the infinite should be incarnate in the finite. Not otherwise than through a divine immanence, however, can I conceive all these finite forms of temporal striving to arise.

What then follows? Does not this follow at once? The finite personality can say:

IMMORTALITY

"In me, as now I am, God is dissatisfied with himself just in so far as now he is partially expressed in me. I am a form of that divine dissatisfaction which constitutes the entire temporal order. This is my link with God, that now I am discontent with the expression of my personality."

In me, then, God is discontented with his own temporal expression. This very discontent I myself am. It constitutes me. This individual thirst for infinity, this personal warfare with my own temporal maladjustment to my own ideal — this is my personality. I am this hatred of my own imperfection, this search for the future deed, this intent to do more than has yet been done. All else about me, — fortune, feeling, hope, fear, joy, sorrow, — these are accidents. These are my clothing, my mere belongings; these constitute the very wilderness of finitude in which I wander. But I — I am essentially the wanderer, whose home is in eternity. And in me God is discontent — discontent with my waywardness — discontent with the little so far done. In me the temporal being, in me now, God is in need, is hungry, is thirsty, is in prison. In me, then, God is dissatisfied. But he is God. He is absolute. Eternity is his. He must be satisfied. In eternity, in the view of the whole temporal process, he is satisfied. In his totality he attains, and he attains what I seek.

This then is, as I conceive, the situation of any finite personality. How is this divine satisfaction attained? I answer, not by ignoring, either now or hereafter, the voluntary individual expression; for it is of the very essence of personality to define its opportunity, its deed, and its meaning, as individual, as insatiable, and unique. And God, too, so defines them, if he knows what personality is. No; the divine satisfaction can be obtained solely through the deeds of the individual. No finite series of these deeds expresses the insatiable demand of the ethical individual for further expression. And this, I take it, is our rational warrant for insisting that every rational person has, in the endless temporal order, an opportunity for an endless series of deeds.

To sum up: Since the time order is the expression of a will continuous with my own, my life cannot ever become a wholly past fact unless my individual will is one that, after some point of time, becomes superfluous for the further temporal expression of the meaning of the whole world life. But as an ethical personality I have an insatiable need for an opportunity to find, to define, and to accomplish my individual and unique duty. This need of mine is God's need in me and of me. Seen, then, from the eternal point of view, my personal life must be an endless series of deeds.

This is a sketch of what I take to be the doctrine of immortality. The reader will observe that I have spoken wholly of will, of deeds, and of opportunity for deeds. I have carefully avoided saying anything about fortune, about future rewards and punishments, about future compensations for present sorrows, about one's rights to meet again one's lost friends, about any of these better known

IMMORTALITY

popular aspects of our topic. As a fact, I pretend to no knowledge about my future fortunes, and to no rights whatever to demand, as a finite personality, any particular sort of good fortune. The doctrine of immortality is to my mind a somewhat stern doctrine. God in eternity wins the conscious satisfaction of my essential personal need. So much I can assert. But my essential personal need is simply for a chance to find out my rational purpose and to do my unique duty. I have no right to demand anything but this. The rest I can leave to a world order which is divine and rational, but which is also plainly a grave and serious order.

.

INDEX

Absolute Pragmatism, 254.
Absolute Truth, 242 ff.
Absolutism, 208 f.
American civilization, 17 f.
Americanism in philosophy, 33.
Aristotle, 241.
Athletic type of morality, 31 f.
Atonement, 135, 138, 155 f., 160, 167, 179 ff.

Baptism, 111.
Bushido, 80.

Calculus of relations, 207.
Carlyle, 39 f.
"Cash values," 34.
Christ, 107, 132 ff., 150 ff., 156, 160, 163 f., 165, 183.
Christianity, Essay III, *passim*.
Christology, 21.
Church, 24, 58, 75, 77, 108, 113, 120 f., 128 f., 160, 170, 182.
Consequences, 34, 36.
Courage, 29.

Darwin and Darwinism, 11.
Dedekind, 210 f., 245 f.
Dewey, 217.
"Dissenter," 108.
Divided self, the, 29.
Divine immanence, 169, 294.

Edwards, Jonathan, 3 ff., 121.
Efficiency, 28, 35, 38.
Emerson, R. W., 3 ff., 8.

Empiricism, 191, 215.
Epimenides, 233.
Eucken, 198.
Euclid, 211, 244 f., 247.
Evil, problem of, 171 ff.
Evolution, doctrine of, 11, 13.
Experience, 22, 34, 37 f., 83, 86, 92, 222 ff., 250.

Faith, 108 ff., 113 f., 124, 126.
Fichte, 42, 188, 192.
Fiske, 12.
Frege, 245.
French Revolution, 200.

Gauss, 212.
God, 105 f., 113 f., 116 f., 134 f., 145 f., 151, 167 ff., 179 ff., 261 ff., 278, 280, 285 f., 295 ff.
Gospel, 135, 140, 142, 161, 169.
Grace, 110, 116, 118.
Greek geometers, 204 f.

Haeckel, 12.
Hegel, 42 f., 188, 192.
Heraclitus, 276.
Hilbert, 210.
Huxley, 12.

Idealism, 189, 197, 254, 272.
Immortality, Essay V, *passim*, 257, 273, 276, 297 f.
Incarnation, 135, 138, 155 f., 160, 163, 167, 179.
Insight, 50, 59 f., 63, 66, 68, 88, 113.

INDEX

Instrumentalism, 194, 209, 214, 221 ff., 235, 253.
Intellectualism, 202, 208 f., 232 f.
Irrationalism, 198.

James, William, Essay I, *passim;* as representative American philosopher, 7; as friend and teacher, 9; as thinker, 10 ff.; as interpreter of evolutionary ideas, 14, 16; his contributions to psychology, 14 ff.; as interpreter of the problems of the American people, 18; his treatment of religious problems, 19 ff.; his attitude toward ethics, 19, 26 ff.; his pragmatism, 32 ff.; his doctrines embodied in "the will to believe," 36 ff.; his polemic against Hegel, 42 f., 210, 217, 224 f.
Job, 64.

Kant, 187, 189, 192, 213, 238, 241, 246, 249.
Kempe, 207.
Kingdom of heaven, 150, 154 f.

Lange, 12.
Logic, 203, 206 f., 208, 234, 238, 250, 252.
Lowell lectures, 32.
Loyalty, Essay II, *passim;* loyalty to college, 49, 75; loyalty and insight, 50, 59 f.; meaning of the term "loyalty," 52 ff.; cause of loyalty, 55 ff., 69 f.; moral law summed up in terms of loyalty, 58 f.; loyalty and modern philosophy of life, 67 ff.; loyalty and reality, 71 ff.; the cause for all the loyal, 77 ff.; loyalty and religion, 90 ff.

Mach, 217.
Mass, 107, 161.
Mathematics, 190, 202, 204, 238 ff., 247, 251 f.
Mechanism, 61 f., 64 f., 66 f., 69, 71, 86 f., 92 f.
Meister Eckhart, 162 f., 164 ff., 180.
Messianic, 141, 147, 149 ff., 154.
Modernism, 199.
Modern philosophy of life, 60 ff., 90.
Monotheism, 122.
Moore, George, 208.
Munsterberg, 86, 258 f., 261, 263, 269, 278 f.

Natural science, 83, 85.
New Realism, 208.
Newton, 218 f., 221.
Nietzsche, 190, 196, 202, 230.
Nogi, General, 80.
Non-Euclidean geometry, 203, 209 f.

Orthodoxy, 108, 123.

Papal condemnation, 22.
Paul, 120.
Pauline charity, 118.
Pauline epistles, 109 f.
Peirce, Charles, 207 f.
"Phänomenologie des Geistes," 188.
Philosophy of action, 39.
Pragmatic method, 33.
Pragmatism, 32 ff., 193, 194 f., 232, 253.
Primitive religion, 103, 106, 120, 122 f., 155.
"Psychical research," 16.

INDEX

Psychology, 14 ff., 189, 216.
Pure Logic, 241 f., 244.

Reality, 66, 69, 71 f., 82, 86, 92, 146.
Redemption, 138.
Reformation, 121.
Relativism, 209, 212, 237.
Religious beliefs, 101 ff., 110 ff., 122 f., 137 f.; practices, 101 ff., 110, 122 f., 126, 137 f.; values, 100, 140.
Religious metaphysics, 145.
Revelation, 93 f.
Roman Catholic Church, 112, 127.
Roman Empire, 148.
Romantic School, 200.
" Rule of Reason," 44.
Russell, 190, 207, 239, 245, 247.

Sacraments, 128.
Schopenhauer, 279.
Skepticism, 88.
Sloth, 29.
Socrates, 195.
Spencer, 11.
Spirit of loyalty, the, 51, 54, 58.
St. Thomas, 262.

Superstition, 62, 65, 68, 83, 90, 92 f., 95.
Symbolic Logic, 241.

Tennyson, 253.
Theory of Assemblages, 203.
Theory of the Categories, 207.
Theory of Knowledge, 187.
Theory of Mathematical Form, 207.
Time, problem of, 257 ff.
Truth, problem of, 33; Essay IV, *passim*.
Tuberculosis, 62.
Tyndall, 12.

Unworldliness, 35.
Upanishads, 195.

" Vital," 100 ff., 105.
Vital elements in any religion, 99 ff., 117 ff., 122; in Christianity, 100 ff., 126 ff., 129 ff., 142 ff., 155, 164 ff., 183.
Voluntarism, 198, 208, 235, 254.
Voluntaristic theory of time, 277 ff.
Von Hartmann, 12.

Zarathustra, 230.

www.ingramcontent.com/pod-product-compliance
Lightning Source LLC
Chambersburg PA
CBHW071939240426
43669CB00048B/2237